W9-CKC-983

THE
BOOK
WARS

BOOKS
BY
JAMES
ATLAS

THE GREAT PRETENDER

DELMORE SCHWARTZ: THE LIFE
OF AN AMERICAN POET

THE BOOK WARS

JAMES ATLAS

WHITTLE DIRECT BOOKS

Portions of chapter 1 reprinted by permission from "Chicago's Grumpy Guru" by James Atlas, January 3, 1988, copyright © by The New York Times Company. Portions of chapters 3 and 4 reprinted by permission from "On Campus: The Battle of the Books" by James Atlas, June 5, 1988, copyright © by The New York Times Company. Portions of chapter 5 reprinted by permission from "Speaking for the Humanities" (ACLS Occasional Paper No. 7), New York, 1989, copyright © by the American Council of Learned Societies.

Photographs: Allan Bloom, Steve Kagan, *People* magazine, page 2; Lynne V. Cheney by Bret Littlehales, page 7; E. D. Hirsch by Bret Littlehales, page 12; Paul de Man, Ken Laffal, page 23; Jane Tompkins by Bret Littlehales, page 32; Frank Lentricchia by Bret Littlehales, page 33; Cleanth Brooks, AP/Wide World Photos (1984), page 33; Stanley Fish by Bret Littlehales, page 34; Thomas Sobol, The Bettmann Archive, page 46; Hilton Kramer by Christopher Barker, page 47; Edmund Wilson, The Bettmann Archive; page 55; Sidney Hook, Victoria Rouse, page 73; Roger Shattuck by Melanie Eve Barocas, page 74; Arthur Schlesinger Jr. by Christopher Barker, page 77; Walter Jackson Bate by Melanie Eve Barocas, page 80.

Library of Congress Catalog Card Number: 90-70484
Atlas, James
The Book Wars
ISBN 0-9624745-3-3
ISSN 1046-364X

The Larger Agenda Series

The Larger Agenda Series presents original short books by distinguished authors on subjects of importance to managers and policymakers in business and the public sector.

The series is edited and published by Whittle Communications L.P., an independent publishing company. A new book appears approximately every other month. The series reflects a broad spectrum of responsible opinions. In each book the opinions expressed are those of the author, not the publisher or the advertiser.

I welcome your comments on this unique endeavor.

William S. Rukeyser
Editor in Chief

CONTENTS

Over 85,000 Federal Express employees around the world share one simple goal: The on-time delivery of your important documents, packages and freight.

THE
WARNING

I n the fall of 1987 I joined the staff of *The New York Times Magazine*. Within a week of my arrival, a senior editor showed up from the third-floor newsroom to suggest that we do a story on Allan Bloom, a philosophy professor at the University of Chicago whose book *The Closing of the American Mind* had been at the top of the bestseller list for months. By the end of that year, it had sold close to a half-million copies. Bloom was America's latest intellectual celebrity: He was interviewed in *Time* magazine and seen on television talk shows. He was also a millionaire, no doubt a rarity among the prestigious members of the Committee on Social Thought.

No one can predict the public's taste. But *The Closing of the American Mind* has turned out to be more than one of those curious American phenomena, a book that captures a moment and acquires fleeting intellectual cachet, like Christopher Lasch's *The Culture of Narcissism* or Charles Reich's *The Greening of America*. Written, its author claimed, to please a few friends, Bloom's book was, and still is, a major event in American life. Three years after its publication, both the book and its author remain objects of intense debate. Bloom was the focus at a symposium entitled "The Humanities and the Question of Values in Education" held at Yale in the spring of 1989. His presence also dominated a conference at Skidmore College sponsored by *Salmagundi*, perhaps the country's leading journal of intellectual opinion. On college bulletin boards around the country, he's frequently announced as a featured speaker. Whether or not *The Closing of the American Mind* will eventually turn out to be "another of those half-read bestsellers that plucks a momentary nerve, materializes fashionably on coffee tables, is rarely read all the way through, and is soon forgotten," as the historian Arthur Schlesinger Jr. has maintained, Bloom's

University of Chicago professor Allan Bloom warned Americans of an impending crisis in universities with *The Closing of the American Mind*, which conjured up a vision of encroaching barbarism.

eloquent polemic is clearly a phenomenon.

It wasn't a book that got raves, to say the least. Classicists faulted Bloom's scholarship, philosophers objected to his interpretations of philosophy, and educators disputed his contention that the universities were in a dreadful state. Commentators on the intellectual left were the most vociferous of all: they charged that Bloom was elitist, reactionary, and undemocratic. *The Closing of the American Mind* was a book that "decent people would be ashamed of having written," declared the writer David Rieff in *The Times Literary Supplement* of London.

What was in this book that provoked such a storm? For one thing, Bloom wasn't so mild-mannered himself. In his survey of the American scene, he found much that was contemptible.

Contemporary students are ignorant, he claimed; they don't read books; they're corrupted in adolescence by primitive rock music. One of Bloom's most notorious images was of a hypothetical 13-year-old boy doing his homework while listening to the "orgasmic rhythms" of a "drag queen" on his Walkman. "In short," he wrote, "life is made into a nonstop, commercially prepackaged masturbation fantasy." But it's not just the young who besmirch America; the culture as a whole is mediocre, "a Disneyland version of the Weimar Republic for the whole family."

The culprit, in Bloom's view, is cultural relativism: the notion that all societies, all cultures, all values are equal. They're not, Bloom insisted. Equality is "a democratic prejudice," an obstacle to the contemplation of higher things. "The real community of man," he concluded, "is the community of those who seek the truth, of the potential knowers, that is, in principle, of all men to the extent they desire to know." In truth, however, "this includes only a few."

How did the university figure in Bloom's scheme of things? His book was subtitled *How Higher Education Has Failed Democracy and Impoverished the Souls of Today's Students*. (Bloom must have gained confidence in his argument as the book made its way through the stages of publication: the subtitle in the galley was *Education and the Crisis of Reason*.) Bloom deplored the low standards that prevail these days on American campuses. Who's to blame? College administrators, who have abdicated their civilizing role by acquiescing to the demand for "relevance." The "radicalization" of the curriculum was, in Bloom's opinion, a plot to discredit the classics—what they call around the University of Chicago the Great Books.

Bloom himself had grown up on those books, and it showed. He didn't wear his scholarship lightly. *The Closing of the American Mind* is an engaging book, crammed with anecdotes and lively personal digressions, but it's not an easy read. The table of contents—"The Nietzscheanization of the Left or Vice Versa," "From Socrates' *Apology* to Heidegger's *Rektoratsrede*"—reflects the density of Bloom's argument. Nor was his thesis entirely new. That the universities were in trouble had been known in the universities for quite a while.

Five years earlier, the eminent biographer and Harvard professor of English Walter Jackson Bate had warned in a famous essay, "The Crisis in English Studies," that the humanities were "plunging into their worst state of crisis since the modern university was formed a century ago." Students of literature no longer had even a rudimentary grasp of the works they used to read as a matter of course, Bate lamented. They knew virtually nothing of history, of foreign languages and literatures, even of their own language and literature.

It was the way Bloom said it that touched a nerve. Instead of supplying statistics about the dwindling capabilities of students, he conjured up a vision of encroaching barbarism. Debunking the 1960s, with its heavy emphasis on equality, democracy, and the rights of the many as opposed to the few, he disparaged with lip-curling verve the cultural vacuity of a generation numbed by rock music: "Mick Jagger played the role in their lives that Napoleon played in the lives of ordinary young Frenchmen throughout the 19th century." What had the 1960s actually produced in the way of culture? Not a whole lot, according to Bloom. "Not a single book of lasting importance was produced in or around the movement." The so-called works of radical philosophy by intellectual gurus such as Herbert Marcuse and Norman O. Brown were spurious adaptations of German philosophy. If there was a decade to celebrate, it was the 1950s, "one of the great periods of the American university," when many of the European scholars who had fled Hitler in great numbers did their most important work: "They initiated us into a tradition that was living and that penetrated the tastes and standards of society at large."

If you happened to believe in Bloom's thesis, this was provocative stuff. If you didn't, it was offensive. Either way, his argument engaged significant issues—what Bloom himself likes to call the Big Questions. "Every educational system has a moral goal that it tries to attain and that informs its curriculum," wrote Bloom. Clearly, that system wasn't working. Moral goals had been sacrificed to new political expediencies; the universities were ruled by special-interest groups, each lobbying for its own discipline—black studies, women's studies, Asian-American studies. "America has no-fault automobile accidents, no-fault divorces, and it is moving with the aid of modern philosophy toward no-fault choices." The new all-inclusive curriculum was like the nature-theater of Oklahoma in Franz Kafka's novel *Amerika*, where "everyone is welcome, everyone can be an artist." In the universities of the 1980s, every culture was welcome.

For Bloom, the implication of all this was clear: the barbarians were at the gate, ready to storm the walled fortress where he did his work. One of the most moving passages in *The Closing of the American Mind* was Bloom's evocation of what the university had meant to him in his youth: "When I was 15 years old I saw the University of Chicago for the first time and somehow sensed that I had discovered my life. I had never before seen, or at least had not noticed, buildings that were evidently dedicated to a higher purpose, not to necessity or utility, not merely to shelter or manufacture or trade, but to something that might be an end in itself." The millionaires— John D. Rockefeller, the McCormicks and other wealthy Chicago families—who had financed a world-class university in their midst, "paid tribute to what they had neglected," Bloom surmised, "whether it was out of a sense of what they themselves had missed, or out of bad conscience about what their lives were exclusively devoted to, or to satisfy the vanity of having their names attached to the enterprise." In the end, it hardly mattered why. The university was there. "Education was an American thing."

Assigned to write a profile of Bloom, I spent an exhilarating week in Hyde Park. I sat in on his class, taking notes like everyone else, while he strode back and forth before the podium, smoking and discoursing in his voluble stammer on Rousseau's *Emile*. Transported back to a world I'd idealized without ever having known, I wasn't disappointed—for once. It was tonic to be out of the pressured realm of New York, where people read only magazines. Browsing in the secondhand bookstores around the university, I was reminded of how much books had once meant to me—not the new releases that I read about in *Publishers' Weekly*, but the old books, the books I'd read in college, for general edification, to satisfy (Bloom has revived the word) my soul.

Yet Bloom inhabited no ivory tower. Following his own passions, scribbling late at night in his Chicago high-rise, he had stumbled upon a hot topic. His book was more than a professor's sour diatribe against rock 'n' roll. It was a warning. What was happening on American campuses, according to Bloom, reflected developments in the culture at large. The Great Books were more than books; they were the essence of all that mattered in Western civilization, the highest expression of our "human desire to know." To produce a generation of students ignorant of those books would have grim consequences in the world beyond the college walls. The decline of educational standards portended the decline of the West. There was a connection between philosophy and politics, between the life of the mind—in Bloom's opinion, the only meaningful life—and the life of the commonwealth. Just as the universities had failed to affirm the supremacy of the values it was their mandate to protect, so had the United States abdicated its role in foreign affairs. "This is the American moment in world history," Bloom cautions, "the one for which we shall forever be judged." Nations are no more relative than cultures; some are destined to lead, others to follow. In short—to use one of Bloom's favorite locutions— we're number one. Or were.

My article appeared in a January 1988 issue of *The New York Times Magazine*, with a photograph of Bloom, cigarette in hand, in one of his elegant French-cut suits. The headline on the cover was CHICAGO'S GRUMPY GURU. But it wasn't until later that year, when I began preliminary work for an article about the curriculum debates that were happening around the country, that I began to sense what was at issue. Walking back to his apartment one afternoon, Bloom had shown me a clipping from that day's *New York Times* that described a flap at Stanford, where a plan was under way to revise the series of Western civilization courses required of freshmen, paring down the core list of classics and substituting works by "women, minorities, and persons of color." "Look at this!" Bloom exclaimed, halting beneath a streetlamp to marvel again at the scrap of paper in his hand. "And people think I exaggerate!"

By that spring, the curriculum was a hot topic. Washington's policymakers seized upon the events at Stanford as an opportunity to attack the universities. Lynne V. Cheney, chairman of the National Endowment for the Humanities, drafted a pamphlet, "Humanities in America," that contained some very bad tidings indeed. Subtitled "A Report to the President, the Congress, and the American People," Cheney's essay made the case that academic departments in history, literature, and the arts were becoming at once overly specialized and lax in their standards. Campus observers had noted an atmosphere of "disarray and isolation," she reported. "They have written of a lost sense of meaning in academic studies." She cited ominous statistics: Between 1966 and 1986 the number of bachelor's degrees awarded by American universities increased by 88 percent; in the humanities, they decreased by 33 percent. It was possible to be graduated from more than 80 percent of four-year colleges and universities without having taken a single course in Western civilization, American history, or a foreign language. "Do students learn how the ideals and practices of our civilization have evolved?" asked Cheney. "Do they take away from their undergraduate years a sense of the interconnection of ideas and events—a framework into which they can fit the learning of a lifetime?" Not the way things stood now. The notion that there existed a hierarchy of knowledge, a cultural tradition made up—in Matthew Arnold's famous phrase—of "the best that has been thought and said," was a thing of the past.

Lynne V. Cheney, chairman of the National Endowment for the Humanities, contends that undergraduates do not learn enough about our civilization to know their place in it.

William Bennett, then secretary of education, was equally dire. "The West is the culture in which we live," he told an audience at Stanford in the spring of 1988. "It has set the moral, political, economic, and social standards for the rest of the world." In bowing to the vocal band of student radicals who had demanded a new, more relevant curriculum, Bennett asserted, "a great university was brought low by the very forces which modern universities came into being to oppose: ignorance, irrationality, and intimidation."

Bennett's outburst, like Bloom's book, created a loud outcry. All over the country, editorials appeared denouncing the sorry developments at Stanford, where students on a 1987 march with Jesse Jackson had chanted, "Hey hey, ho ho, Western culture's gotta go." Universities in America have always been viewed with a certain amount of suspicion, idealized as places of higher learning but not entirely respected; they're too far from the sources of wealth and power. But at least they were tolerated as a supposedly civilizing influence. Now it seemed they had a very different mission. The defenders of high culture were in the real world, in politics and government; the philistines were in the university. Bloom and Bennett became a synecdoche for the old guard: standard-bearers opposed to curriculum reform and the menace to Western culture it represented. (In the academic world, they were known as the Killer B's.)

On campus, meanwhile, administrators were scrambling to meet the demand for courses that would represent a veritable rainbow coalition of constituencies. At Berkeley, the cradle of student radicalism during the 1960s, home of the original Free-Speech Movement, the faculty voted to adopt a new requirement. Freshmen or sophomores would have to pass a one-semester course focusing on at least three out of five ethnic groups: African-Americans, Latinos, Asian-Americans, Native Americans, and European-Americans.

The curricular debate was more than a matter of placating various ethnic groups. In 1988 the Yale professor and critic Paul de Man made posthumous headlines when it was discovered that he had written a number of antisemitic articles for Nazi-controlled periodicals in Belgium during World War II. In his new incarnation as an Ivy League academic, de Man became one of the most influential proponents in the universities of deconstructionism, a literary method that insists upon the "indeterminacy of the text." Language is incapable of saying what it means to say, claim the deconstructionists; the author invariably reveals motives, or intentions, that elude his conscious design; the act of critical interpretation is fatally flawed by the reader's own presuppositions, or "blindness." Language and literature can never be put in the service of truth because it is impossible to determine what the truth is: a work of art is beyond interpretation.

Francis Fukuyama, a State Department official, also generated a vast amount of coverage in the press with his article "The End of History?" Published in *The National Interest*, the essay was an effort to translate Bloom's ideas into the realm of politics. To all appearances, Fukuyama was optimistic; in the 20th century, he argued, the forces of totalitarianism have been decisively conquered by the United States and its allies, which represent the final embodiment of history—"that is, the end point of mankind's ideological evolution and the universalization of Western liberal democracy." In other words, we win.

Not so fast. The end of history, according to Fukuyama, would be "a very sad time." The "emptiness at the core of liberalism" would become drearily apparent. The triumph of democracy would usher in a "consumerist culture" purveying rock music around the world. Where had I heard this rhetoric before? It turned out that Fukuyama had been a student of Bloom's at Cornell. He had also been a graduate student in comparative literature at Yale, where he studied with Paul de Man.

From deconstructionism to the highest levels of government, from literary theory to foreign policy—I was beginning to get the drift. The attack on the meaning of a literary text—on its authority—was analogous to the attack on political authority that had begun in the 1960s. Deconstructionism had its origin in Continental philosophy; so did the campus riots of the 1960s, at least in Bloom's version of things. America may have triumphed in the economic and military spheres, but it had failed in the educational sphere. Indeed, the universities were busy working to undermine the very values for which they had once stood. And it wasn't just the universities. The same thing was happening everywhere. For all its prosperity, America was a nation in spiritual decline. It was hollow at the core.

"What do Shakespeare and Milton have to do with solving our problems?" Bloom asks in *The Closing of the American Mind*. As it happens, everything.

Federal Express is the world's largest full-service all-cargo airline.
We offer more planes, vans and overseas routes—and more overseas
shipping experts—than ever before.

CULTURAL ILLITERACY

At first glance, E. D. Hirsch's *Cultural Literacy* seemed as unlikely a bestseller as *The Closing of the American Mind*. Originally a lecture given before the Modern Language Association, it was published as an essay in *The American Scholar* in 1983. "I received a letter from Robert Payton, president of the Exxon Education Foundation," Hirsch wrote in the introduction to his book, "encouraging me to start acting on my perceptions rather than just writing them down."

Spurred on by an Exxon grant, Hirsch began to compile his now-famous list of the "items" that, if known and mastered, would enable this and future generations of students to attain cultural literacy. In 1987 he published his book, which instantly made the bestseller list; for 40 weeks it was second only to Bloom's. The paperback has sold 600,000 copies. Hirsch, a professor of English at the University of Virginia and a scholar of 18th-century literature, has become the latest representative of that new American type, the academic celebrity.

What is cultural literacy? The answer is simply put in the subtitle of Hirsch's book: *What Every American Needs to Know*. By "culture" Hirsch doesn't mean "high culture," but "basic information," the names and events that enable us to decipher the world. In order to function in society, to work and to communicate, he argues, people need to possess a certain number of facts about their own history. The key events in our past, the key phrases in our literature, are in themselves a kind of language, a code that educated people decipher in their daily lives without even knowing it. Hirsch reminisces about his father, an old-fashioned businessman who used to quote Shakespeare in his correspondence and often used the phrase

E. D. Hirsch, a professor of English at the University of Virginia and author of *Cultural Literacy*, is working to establish a national curriculum that will address inequities in inner-city schools.

"There is a tide"—shorthand for "There is a tide in the affairs of men/Which taken at the flood leads on to fortune" from *Julius Caesar*—to illustrate how one knows intuitively when to buy or sell. "To persuade somebody that your recommendation is wise and well founded, you have to give lots of reasons and cite known examples and authorities," wrote Hirsch. "My father accomplished that and more in four words, which made quoting Shakespeare as effective as any efficiency consultant could wish."

For Bloom, the decline of educational standards can be traced to the decline of philosophy (a word he uses to mean the humanities in general); to ignore the classics is ultimately to weaken the very foundations of our society. Hirsch is more pragmatic. For him, the purpose of education isn't to produce a handful of Greek scholars who can preserve the great intellectual traditions of the West, as Allan Bloom would have it, but to prepare us for the complex social transactions of everyday life. It's not a nation of English professors that Hirsch aspires to create, but a nation in which business people and politicians are literate enough to negotiate effectively in the world. "High stakes," he writes, are involved in the curriculum debate:

> . . . breaking the cycle of illiteracy for deprived children; raising the living standard of families who have been illiterate; making our country more competitive in international markets; achieving greater social justice; enabling all citizens to participate in the political process; bringing us closer to the Ciceronian ideal of universal public discourse—in short, achieving fundamental goals of the founders at the birth of the republic.

There's nothing abstract about this imperative. Behind Hirsch's high-minded rhetoric is a pretty straightforward message: You can't expect people to grasp the basic principles of democracy unless they know what those principles are. And you can't expect them to function effectively in the world unless they're literate.

A front-page article in the September 25, 1989, *New York Times* bore the headline IMPENDING U.S. JOBS 'DISASTER': WORK FORCE UNQUALIFIED TO WORK. The article quoted business executives like David T. Kearns, chairman of Xerox Corporation, who predicted "the makings of a national disaster," and James E. Burke, chief executive officer of Johnson & Johnson, who spoke of "the American dream turned nightmare." There are jobs out there, but there aren't enough qualified people to fill them. Graduating students lack even the basic skills required to work on an assembly line, let alone the kind of skills necessary for clerical or white-collar jobs. Computer technology has made these jobs more complicated than they were a decade ago; they demand more training—a phenomenon known as upskilling. Yet the average young adult between the ages of 21 and 25 reads at a level well below what most available jobs demand. "We cannot compete in a world-class economy without a world-class work force," the *Times* quoted Kearns, "and we cannot have a world-class work force without world-class schools."

Thisdour assessment is supported by the facts. In a 1988 survey of high school students' scientific achievement level prepared by the International Association for the Evaluation of Educational Achievement, the United States ranked third-to-last out of 15 developed nations; in a 1970 survey, the U.S. had ranked seventh. It's not that other nations have improved in terms of education; we have deteriorated. U.S. Scholastic Aptitude Test (SAT) scores have declined precipitously over the last decade: from 1972 to 1984, 56 percent fewer students scored over 600 and 73 percent fewer scored over 650. A 1983 report by the National Commission on Excellence in Education stated, "For the first time in the history of our country, the educational skills of one generation will not surpass, will not equal, will not even approach those of their parents."

Americans know less than ever. Hirsch's book is full of frightening statistics: Two-thirds of 17-year-olds weren't aware that the Civil War occurred between 1850 and 1900. Nearly half couldn't identify Stalin; nearly one-fourth couldn't identify Churchill. When Hirsch's son, a high school Latin teacher, asked his class to name an epic poem by Homer, one student volunteered "The Alamo?" Another, informed that Latin was no longer spoken, asked, "What do they speak in Latin America?" Hirsch reported in *The New York Review of Books* on a conference of college deans where he had been regaled with "a chorus of anecdotes" about the decline in literacy among entering freshmen. "To these administrators," Hirsch wrote, "the debate over Stanford University's required courses seemed interesting but less than momentous when compared with the problem of preparing students to participate intelligently in any university-level curriculum."

Reports from the English-composition front confirm the deans' pessimism. Jerry Doolittle, an English instructor at Harvard, designed a quiz for his freshmen students to determine their level of literacy. They were given 20 statements and

THE U.S. SCORES LOW IN SCIENTIFIC ACHIEVEMENT

Ranking by international standardized test scores of 14-year-olds.

1. Hungary
2. Japan
3. Netherlands
4. Canada
5. Finland
6. Sweden
7. Poland
8. Norway
9. Australia
10. England
11. Singapore, Thailand, United States
14. Hong Kong
15. Philippines

SOURCE: INTERNATIONAL ASSOCIATION FOR THE EVALUATION OF EDUCATIONAL ACHIEVEMENT, 1988

were asked to fill in the blanks. Among the sample questions were the following:

I think that I shall never see a poem _____ (four words)

Quoth the raven, _____ (one word)

A jug of wine, a loaf of bread and _____ (one word)

The average score was seven out of 20—a figure somewhat inflated, Doolittle confessed, by two statements that everyone in the class completed correctly: "Winston tastes good, like a _____" (two words) and "This Bud's for _____" (one word). And this was Harvard!

According to Richard Marius, director of Harvard's Expository Writing Program, arriving freshmen are so woefully deficient in the basic skills of reading and writing that a remedial course is required just to get them to the point where their peers would have been a generation ago. "This generation does not read," Marius laments in *Teaching Literature: What Is Needed Now*. They're unfamiliar with the Bible, Shakespeare, Milton; they don't even know the Gettysburg Address: "they are strangers not only to those points of reference that might help them navigate the literary sea, but also to the underlying cadences that have governed the development of written English. They cannot write because they have not read and they cannot hear."

How to remedy the situation? College is too late, in Hirsch's view. Cultural illiteracy is a function of inadequate early schooling. Inner-city public schools lag far behind those in the suburbs, which means that minorities and poor children are at a disadvantage when it comes to acquiring the reading skills necessary to keep up with more privileged students. By the time students reach the third or fourth grade, their teachers can identify those who will drop out. By the time they're in high school, these students have already fallen hopelessly behind, creating an educational division between the haves and the have-nots.

Education in this country has become a privilege rather than a right. Whole populations have been denied this right, and the consequences are now upon us. As Joe Kellman, a Chicago businessman who founded a private school for slum children, put it, "If we don't figure out how to educate blacks and Hispanics in our inner cities, then we can kiss our democratic society goodbye."

Hirsch is working virtually single-handedly to establish a curriculum that will address this terrible inequity. He is founder and president of the Cultural Literacy Foundation, whose many activities include publishing a newsletter and offering a provisional list of what different people should know at different grade levels. To help achieve this goal, he has enlisted a network of some 800 schools in all 50 states and two protectorates. His *Dictionary of Cultural Literacy* is in the stores, and he is at work on a six-volume textbook designed to teach students the rudiments of American history, the great works of English and American literature, and the sciences. Hirsch writes, "The effort to develop a standard sequence of core knowledge is, to put it bluntly, absolutely essential to effective educational reform in the United States." His ambition is to have this textbook adopted in classrooms throughout the land.

It makes sense. No society can survive for long without a consensus about what that society stands for, what it is. Right now, there's no consensus—worse, the very notion of consensus is under attack. We no longer agree to disagree. Even to propose that we establish a curriculum is to enforce the will of an elite. As E. D. Hirsch's Shakespeare-quoting father might have put it, echoing Hamlet, "There is nothing either good or bad but thinking makes it so."

We've made tens of millions of international air express and
air freight deliveries. Federal Express has the experience to handle
your dutiable and document shipments overseas.

In addition to our hub in Memphis, Federal Express
has 12 other hubs strategically located domestically and abroad
to quickly process your air express and freight shipments.

THE BIG BOYS

The philosopher George Santayana was once asked which books young people ought to read. It didn't matter, he replied, as long as they read the same ones. Generations of college students followed his advice. In the standard introductory course to Western civ you read some Greek philosophy, the Bible, St. Augustine, Machiavelli, Rousseau, Marx, and John Stuart Mill. If it was a literature course, you read Chaucer, Shakespeare, Milton, the Romantic poets, the Victorian novelists . . . and so on, century by century, masterpiece by masterpiece, until you'd read (or browsed through) the corpus. The best that has been thought and said.

The best, like everything else, was susceptible to fashion. Occasional disputes broke out, reputations waxed and waned. T. S. Eliot restored the luster of the 17th-century metaphysical poets; the literary critic Malcolm Cowley promoted Faulkner; there was a Henry James revival. For the most part, though, you were either on the syllabus or off the syllabus.

What *is* the best that has been thought and said? Gerald

Graff, a professor of English at Northwestern University and one of the most articulate commentators on the curriculum debate, observes that the trouble with this "Matthew Arnold view of literature and culture" is that there never was any consensus about what it meant to be educated in our society. The idea of literature as a fixed and immutable canon—the Great Books, the Five-Foot Shelf—is a historical illusion. "Canon-busting is nothing new," says Graff. "There have always been politics. Teaching Shakespeare instead of the classics was a radical innovation."

Teaching literature was once an innovation. Until the late 19th century, philology—the linguistic analysis of literature—was the closest thing to literary studies in the university. Rhetoric, oratory, Greek, and Latin dominated the syllabus. It wasn't until about the 1880s that literature as we now know it became a proper subject of study, and even then scholars were mostly textual exegetes, devoted to the preparation of new editions of the classics. The idea that literature could serve as a guide to the conduct of life, an interpretation of culture, had no place in the university. This was a field reserved for critics: generalists like Henry Wadsworth Longfellow and James Russell Lowell, who wrote for wide-circulation magazines and decried the professionalism of their academic colleagues.

Literature as linguistics—the "philological syndicate," as Harry Levin, a former professor of comparative literature at Harvard, has described it—was eventually superseded by the New Criticism of poet-critics like John Crowe Ransom and Allen Tate, who taught in universities and were influential in the literary world. They, too, were devoted to close reading, or analysis, of texts; but they ventured beyond the classics. Their most famous essays are about the English poets, and those were the poets they taught. By the 1940s, literature as it was studied by undergraduates meant English and American literature with a handful of works in translation thrown in.

When I was a freshman at Harvard in 1967, the English literature courses listed in the catalog were more or less the same ones that had been offered for decades (and so were the professors): "Biblical Symbolism in English Literature," "English Poetry and Prose of the Romantic Period," "English Poetry:

Dryden to Wordsworth," "The Nineteenth-Century English Novel." There were some hip courses, like "The Modern Sensibility," which covered Yeats and Freud; *Love's Body* by Norman O. Brown; *Tristes Tropiques*, the autobiography of Claude Lévi-Strauss; and Ludwig Wittgenstein's *Tractatus*. But you also needed a certain number of credits in English literature to get a degree, you needed to know at least one foreign language, and you had to demonstrate some acquaintance with *The Norton Anthology of English Literature*.

Even then, there was spirited debate about the purpose of education—not only what books a student ought to read, but what kinds of values they were meant to inculcate. The question, as Lionel Trilling framed it in a prophetic lecture, "The Uncertain Future of the Humanistic Educational Ideal," was a practical one: "What is best for young minds to be engaged by, how they may best be shaped through what they read—or look at or listen to—and think about." At Columbia, where Trilling studied and where he taught for a half-century, the Great Books Program, as it came to be known there, was firmly enshrined. The study of the "whole man"—that is to say, history, ethics, philosophy, as well as literature—was standard procedure. ("No one then thought of the necessity of saying the 'whole person,'" Trilling noted dryly.)

By the 1960s, the whole-man idea had been scaled down considerably. It was possible to earn a bachelor of arts degree without a lot of sweat. I recall my panic when called upon in a final exam to discuss works from the four principal phases of Shakespeare's career. Having consulted previous exams—they were available in the library for that purpose—I had taken my cue from the Shakespeare question of the year before and boned up on one play from each of the four principal genres: comedy, tragedy, history, and romance. I wrote about genre—and got a decent grade. The experience was a vivid confirmation that not much was expected of us. If you happened to read a few of the books they asked you to read, fine. If not, also fine.

What my classmates and I managed to learn in those four years couldn't begin to compare with the knowledge absorbed by earlier generations of students, for whom the study of literature included the study of Greek and Latin classics in the original. But at least the idea of general education was intact. No one disputed that there were Great Books. No one doubted that it was a good thing to have some grasp of what Western culture was all about.

The curriculum wasn't an issue then. Our demands (as we called them at Harvard) were explicitly political. They focused on the draft, ROTC, the Vietnam War, the ethics of military research and the universities' investment policies, the grievances of the (usually poor and black) communities on their perimeters. Not that the members of Students for a Democratic Society (SDS), the primary organization of campus radicals, were doctrinaire Marxists; their meetings and demonstrations were often suffused with a distinctly countercultural aura. STRIKE BECAUSE THERE'S NO POETRY IN YOUR LIFE, read the motto on posters and T-shirts adorned with a clenched red fist in the spring of 1969. But politics was an extracurricular activity; in the library, we still read Locke and Hobbes.

The faculty grasped the implications of the student movement more quickly than did its instigators. "The past five years have been, for American universities, the most dramatic in our history," wrote Daniel Bell and Irving Kristol in their preface to *Confrontation: The Student Rebellion and the University* (1969). Dramatic and devastating, from their point of view: what was happening in that turbulent era was nothing less than the destruction of the university and of the civilization whose noblest monuments of learning it was the university's mandate to preserve. "Not since the civil conflict of a century ago has this country, as I see it, been in such great danger," warned the American diplomat George Kennan in a 1968 essay prompted by the events at Columbia. The ideals of "commitment, duty, self-restraint" that higher education was supposed to encourage in the young had been sacrificed, said Kennan, in the name of a spurious personal freedom masquerading as politics.

The danger passed. By the mid-1970s, the campus violence of a few years before was history. The gun-toting black students who occupied an administration building at Cornell in 1969 had put away their weapons; SDS had become a fringe group on the left. Within a few years, half a decade if that, the momentous events my generation witnessed—the March on Washington, the Chicago convention of 1968—had become oddly remote. The Republicans were back in office, and the public was transfixed by the Watergate hearings. It was as if the 1960s had never happened.

Yet the student movement left its mark. Afro-American departments were a feature of most universities; ROTC was gone, or on the way out; the Vietnam War was over. On campus, the most enduring legacy of that decade was to be found in the curriculum. "During the '60s I sat on various committees at Cornell and continuously and futilely voted against dropping one requirement after the next," Bloom recalled. "The old core curriculum—according to which every student in the college had to take a smattering of courses in the major divisions of knowledge—was abandoned." What was left was "a threadbare reminiscence of the unity of knowledge" that had been the university's original purpose and ideal.

Yale professor Paul de Man was a leading proponent of deconstructionism—the questioning of the literal meaning of literary works—which became by the 1970s the dominant mode of criticism.

At least it was a reminiscence. In the aftermath of the 1960s, students of literature were indoctrinated with a method that was, if anything, *more* esoteric than the New Criticism it supplanted: deconstructionism. This would become the dominant mode of literary criticism and practice within the university. By the 1970s, no one was just reading anymore; everyone was deconstructing.

There was nothing simple about this new discipline. Indeed, its vocabulary was so difficult, so willfully abstract, that only initiates could decipher its primary "texts" (or books, as they used to be known). "As seen from the public perspective of literary journalists and literary critics, the disputes among literary theorists more and more appear to be like quarrels among theologians, at the furthest remove from any reality or practicality," began one of Paul de Man's late essays, entitled "Hypogram and Inscription." The same essay ended with a sentence that seemed as if it had been designed to confirm the suspicions of the very public that de Man belittled (if any representative of it got that far): "Inscription is neither a figure, nor a sign, nor a cognition, nor a desire, nor a hypogram, nor a matrix, yet no theory of reading or of poetry can achieve consistency if it responds to its powers only by a figural invasion which, in this case, takes the subtly effective form of evading the figural." In other words (I think), works of literature don't necessarily say what they intend to say.

What was radical about this new critical discipline was its premise: namely, that the impulse to interpret works of literature is itself political. Literary criticism is "strategic, a violent and bloody act," according to de Man. To deconstruct a text is to question its literal meaning, the validity of its authorial point of view—to challenge its intent. "All language is about language," de Man insisted. Interpreting Shelley's poem "The Triumph of Life," he found that its imagery was largely unconscious, its logic impaired. The poem didn't track. Shelley's description of dawn made it seem as if that natural phenomenon, "the most continuous and gradual event in nature," happened all at once: ". . . the sun sprang forth." The image, noted de Man, is "brusque and unmotivated." How could it be otherwise? "Language posits and language means (since it articulates), but language cannot posit meaning; it can only reiterate (or reflect) it in its reconfirmed falsehood." In other words, Shelley didn't know what he was doing.

Yet even deconstructionism, subversive as it was, concentrated its deconstructive—that is to say, its destructive—energies on traditional works. The texts de Man taught—Wordsworth, Blake, Yeats—were the same ones an earlier generation of critics had interpreted in its own fashion. It wasn't the curriculum that had changed; it was our way of reading the books that composed it.

It wasn't until the mid-1980s that real trouble broke out. My first intimation of it was in the academic journals: I kept stumbling across references to the *canon*. Originally, the word referred to those works that the church considered part of the Bible; now, apparently, it had a new meaning. *PMLA*, the journal of the Modern Language Association, proposed an

With over 100,000 computer terminals—the largest
private communications network in the world—the status of your
package is just a phone call away.

Every business day, over 2,200 FAA-certified Federal Express pilots fly nearly 400,000 miles to deliver your documents, packages and freight around the world.

issue on "the idea of the literary canon in relation to concepts of judgment, taste, and value." In the spring of 1988, the Princeton English department held a symposium entitled "Masterpieces: Canonizing the Literary."

Canon formation, canon revision, canonicity: the mysterious, often indecipherable language of criticism had yielded a whole new terminology. What was this canon? The books that constituted the intellectual heritage of educated Americans, that had officially been defined as great. The kind of books you read, say, in Columbia's famed lit hum course, virtually unchanged since 1937: Homer, Plato, Dante, Milton. The masterpieces of Western civilization. The Big Boys.

In the academic world, I kept hearing, the canon was a hot issue. "Everything these days has to do with the canon," one of my campus sources reported. Then came Bloom and Bennett. By the spring of 1988, "canon politics" was in the news. "From Western lit to Westerns as lit," joked *The Wall Street Journal* in a piece about some English professors down at Duke who were teaching *The Godfather* (both the book and the movie), *E.T.*, and the novels of Louis L'Amour. An article in *The New York Times* entitled "U.S. Literature: Canon Under Siege" quoted a heretical brigade of academics who were fed up with literary-value hierarchies. Why should Melville and Emerson dominate the syllabus? argued renegade professors from Princeton and Duke. What about Zora Neale Hurston, a heroine of the Harlem renaissance? What about Harriet Beecher Stowe? "It's no different from choosing between a hoagie and a pizza," explained Houston Baker, a professor of literature at the University of Pennsylvania.

Up at Harvard, nothing had changed in Warren House, the colonial clapboard dwelling across from the student union, where I'd gone for tutorials with Robert Fitzgerald, the late Boylston Professor of English and translator of the *Odyssey*, 20 years ago. The stuffy, low-ceilinged rooms, with their worn Persian carpets and book-crammed mahogany shelves, were just as I remembered them. Only the catalog had changed. "Courses of Instruction 1988-1989" was as bewildering a volume as any text by Paul de Man. On the cover was that reassuring logo: VERITAS. I turned to the listings under

English and American Literature and Language. There was "Old English Literature in Translation," still taught by the playwright and Harvard legend William Alfred. There was "The Age of Johnson" and "English Romantic Poetry." But what was this? "Virginia Woolf and Toni Morrison"? A course on Southern fiction that included Ellen Gilchrist and Alice Walker? "Modern American Poetry," taught by no less an authority than the distinguished critic Helen Vendler, that offered readings in Dave Smith, Jorie Graham, and Rita Dove?

It wasn't only the new—in some cases unknown—names that stopped me. The course descriptions were just as strange. My eye fell upon "Literature and Human Suffering," a course on "Tolstoy, Hardy, Melville, Douglass, Solzhenitsyn, and writers dealing with slavery and the Holocaust." Then there was "Representations of Family and Kinship in the 18th-Century Novel," described as "an investigation of the treatment of family relations and sexuality," of "incest as a narrative trope." "The Politics of Childbirth and Childhood in Anglo-American Literature" would consider *Alice in Wonderland, The Land of Oz,* and *The Bluest Eye* by Toni Morrison. Even the traditional courses promised untraditional approaches: "Problems in Shakespearean Interpretation," billed as an advanced course, for instance, would address "questions opened by feminism, new historicism, materialism, deconstruction, psychoanalysis, and other post-structuralist ways of reading and interpreting."

Amazing! In just two decades, the teaching of literature—the values it was supposed to inculcate, the questions it was supposed to answer, the very books themselves—had been transformed. What mattered now was *contextualization*: establishing a work in its historical context. Literature as sociology—that was the new game. Consider, for instance, English 90cd, "Literature, Politics, and the English Revolution": " . . . an examination of the rich variety of texts—literary, sub-literary, political—which refract in diverse ways the experience and culture of Interregnum England."

I read on: "Women and Culture in Victorian Society," "Black and White in American Culture," "Innocence and

Violence in America," "The Rise of Mass Culture." It all sounded very interesting. The only thing missing was the books.

Well, what of it? There was a long tradition of studying literature in this way. Marx and his disciples had contributed a great deal in the line of literary criticism, from *Leon Trotsky on Literature and Art* to the writings of Walter Benjamin, from Hannah Arendt to Edward Said. Edmund Wilson, by consensus America's greatest literary critic, was a diligent historian; his most important books, *To the Finland Station* and *Patriotic Gore*, are models of how to write about literature against the backdrop of history.

Only it wasn't just history that dominated literature now; it was politics. The whole idea behind the new curriculum, I gathered from my own close reading of the Harvard catalog, was to recognize and identify the ideological forces that produced a work of art. It was the context they were looking at, what a book—any book—said about society. "Modern experimental novels considered as explorations of shifting racial and sexual relations." "An investigation of the treatment of family relations and sexuality in a number of 18th-century novels." "Selected autobiographies raise issues of nationalism, race, gender, and American self-styling. . . . "

I thought of a line from Yeats (was he still taught?): "The world is changed, changed utterly."

DADS,^{SM} our in-truck computer terminal, is used by our couriers
to enter the location of your package into COSMOS,$^®$
our worldwide tracking system.

THE NEW CANONISTS

CHAPTER
4

On the shelves in Jane Tompkins's office at Duke are rows of 19th-century novels; she is one of the few who reads them now. Her book *Sensational Designs: The Cultural Work of American Fiction 1790-1860* is a brilliant exhumation of what she considers lost masterpieces, the history of a different American literature from the one I read in college 20 years ago.

Writers like Charles Brockden Brown, Harriet Beecher Stowe, and Susan Warner still deserve an audience, Tompkins argues with considerable persuasiveness. If they're no longer read, it's because our values have changed. The way to read these books is from the vantage of the past. Only by reconstructing the culture in which they were written and the audience to whom they were addressed can we learn to appreciate their intrinsic worth and see them for what they are: "man-made, historically produced objects" whose reputations were created in their day by a powerful literary establishment. In other words, the Great Books aren't the only books.

Tompkins is one of the jewels in the crown of Duke's English department, which in the last few years has assembled a faculty that can now claim to rival any in the country. Attracted by salaries that in some cases approach six figures and a university willing to let them teach pretty much whatever interests them, the new recruits compose a formidable team: Frank Lentricchia, the author of *After the New Criticism* and other works; Fredric Jameson, probably the foremost Marxist critic in the country; Barbara Herrnstein Smith, a former president of the Modern Language Association; and Tompkins's husband, Stanley Fish, chairman of the department. (Duke is known in academic circles as the Fish Tank.)

Canon revision is in full swing down at Duke, where

Jane Tompkins, a professor of English at Duke, says if the Great Books are no longer read, it's because our values have changed.

students lounge about the manicured quad of the imitation-Cotswold campus, and the magnolias blossom in the spring. In the Duke catalog, the English department lists, besides the usual offerings in Chaucer and Shakespeare, courses entitled "American Popular Culture," "Advertising and Society," "Television, Technology, and Culture."

Lentricchia teaches a course entitled "Paranoia, Politics, and Other Pleasures" that focuses on the works of Joan Didion, Don DeLillo, and Michel Foucault. Tompkins, an avid reader of contemporary fiction—on a shelf in her office I spotted copies of *Princess Daisy* and *Valley of the Dolls*—is teaching all kinds of things, from a course on American literature and culture in the 1850s to one called "Home on the Range: The Western in American Culture."

Tompkins talks about her work with a rhetorical intensity that reminds me of the fervent Students for a Democratic Society types I used to know in college. Like so many of those in the vanguard of the new canonical insurrection, she is a child of the '60s and a dedicated feminist. In *Sensational Designs*, she recounts how she gradually became aware of herself as a woman working in a "male-dominated scholarly tradition that controls both the canon of American literature and the critical perspective that interprets the canon for society." The writers offered up as classics didn't speak to Tompkins; they didn't address her own experience.

"If you look at the names on Butler Library up at Columbia, they're all white males," she notes one afternoon over lunch in the faculty dining hall. "We wanted to talk about civil rights in the classroom, to prove that literature wasn't a sacred icon above the heat and dust of conflict."

The English-literature syllabus, Tompkins and her colleagues on other campuses discovered, was a potential instrument of change: "This is where it all came out in the wash." By the 1970s, women's studies majors had been installed on college campuses across the land. Books on gender, race, and ethnicity poured from the university presses. Seminars were offered in Native American literature, Hispanic literature, and Asian-American literature. "It wasn't only women we'd neglected," says Marjorie Garber, director of the Harvard Center for Literary and Cultural Studies. "It was the whole third world."

The ideology behind these challenges to the canon is as obvious as the vanity plates on Frank Lentricchia's old Dodge: GO LEFT. Pick up any recent academic journal and you'll find it packed with articles on "Maidens, Maps, and Mines: The Reinvention of Patriarchy in Colonial South Africa" or "Dominance, Hegemony, and the Modes of Minority Discourse." The critical vocabulary of the 1980s bristles with militant neologisms: *Eurocentrism, phallocentrism, logophallocentrism* (why not *Europhallologocentrism*?). "This is not an intellectual agenda; it is a political agenda," former secretary of education Bennett declared.

Why should a revolutionary curricular struggle be happening at a time when radical politics in America is virtually extinct? Walk into any classroom and you'll find the answer. Enormous sociological changes have occurred in American universities over the last 20 years; the ethnic profile of both

Changing styles in the English departments: Yale's eminent Cleanth Brooks (above), Frank Lentricchia of Duke (left).

students and faculty has undergone a dramatic transformation. There's a higher proportion of minorities in college than ever before. By the end of this century, Hispanic, black, and Asian-American undergraduates at Stanford may well outnumber whites. Their professors, many of whom were on the barricades in the 1960s, are now up for tenure.

"It's a demographic phenomenon," Jane Tompkins says. "There are women, Jews, Italians teaching literature in universities. The people who are teaching now don't look the way professors used to look. Frank Lentricchia doesn't look like Cleanth Brooks."

I have never seen Cleanth Brooks, the eminent Yale professor emeritus, but I can imagine him striding across campus in a conservative gray suit and neat bow tie—not at all the way Frank Lentricchia looks. The photograph on the book jacket of *Criticism and Social Change* shows a guy in a sports shirt, posed against a graffiti-scarred wall—"the Dirty Harry of contemporary critical theory," a reviewer in *The Village Voice* called him.

In person, Lentricchia is a lot less intimidating. I found him mild-mannered, easygoing, and surprisingly conventional in his approach to literature. Standing before his modern-poetry class in a faded blue work shirt open at the neck, he made his way through *The Waste Land* just the way professors used to, line by line, pointing out the buried allusions to Ovid and Dante, Marvell and Verlaine.

Stanley Fish, chairman of the Duke English department ("the Fish Tank"), advocates teaching literature that reflects the experience of minority groups: "Assimilation is a betrayal."

His work is densely theoretical, yet there's nothing doctrinaire about it. What comes through is a devotion to the classics that is more visceral than abstract. "I'm interested in social issues as they bear on literature. But what really interests me is the mainline stuff, like Faulkner," he says after class, popping open a beer—no sherry—on the porch of his comfortable home in the nearby town of Hillsboro. "I'm too American to be a Marxist."

One afternoon I talked with Stanley Fish in his newly renovated office in the Allen Building. Fish had on slacks and a sports jacket, but he didn't look any more like Cleanth Brooks, or my image of Cleanth Brooks, than Frank Lentricchia does. He's never been at ease with the T. S. Eliot tradition, he said, though he's one of the leading Milton scholars in America.

Now 52, Fish is maybe a decade older than the generation of radical scholars that came of age in the 1960s; but like many of them, he discovered his vocation largely on his own. "You come from a background where there were no books, the son and daughter of immigrants," he says. In such a world, Milton was a first name.

For American writers who grew up in the Depression, the art critic Clement Greenberg once noted, literature offered "a means of flight from the restriction and squalor of the Brooklyns and Bronxes to the wide-open world which rewards the successful fugitive with space, importance, and wealth." Making it in those days meant making it on others' terms: in this case, the terms established by tradition-minded English departments dominated by white Anglo-Saxon Protestants, which even in the 1940s looked with skeptical distaste upon the Jewish assistant professors who were trying to storm the gates.

Diana Trilling has written movingly about the humiliation her celebrated husband, Lionel, suffered at the beginning of his career, when he was briefly banished from Columbia by the English department on the grounds that he was "a Freudian, a Marxist, and a Jew." There was nothing subversive about Trilling's ambition; for him, as for Jewish critics like Philip Rahv and Harry Levin, literature was an escape from ethnic identity, not an affirmation of it.

Fish and his radical colleagues are no less ambitious. They, too, aspire to "space, importance, and wealth," but on their own terms. Frank Lentricchia has a swimming pool in his back yard. In his work, though, he writes openly and with unashamed ardor, in the autobiographical fashion of the day, about his Italian-American origins, his grandfather in Utica, and his working-class dad. "To become an intellectual from this kind of background means typically to try to forget where you've come from," he writes in *Criticism and Social Change*. It means becoming "a cosmopolitan gentleman of the world of letters, philosophy, and art."

That's not Lentricchia's style. For the scholars of his generation, it's no longer a matter of proving their claim on literature; that struggle has been won. What they're demanding now is a literature that reflects their experience, a literature of their own. "Assimilation is a betrayal," says Fish. "The whole idea of 'Americanness' has been thrown in question."

A recent anthology published by the Graywolf Press in St. Paul, Minnesota, confirms this trend. Entitled *Multi-Cultural Literacy: Opening the American Mind*, it makes deliberate reference to the two best-selling books that brought the revolution in the humanities to the attention of a larger public: Bloom's *Closing of the American Mind* and Hirsch's *Cultural Literacy*. *Multi-Cultural Literacy* is a populist anthology, an alternative to the "institutionalized racism" of the curriculum, with its "white, male, academic, eastern U.S., Eurocentric bias." Where on Hirsch's list of "What Every American Needs to Know" is the *Bhagavad Gita*? Where is *One Hundred Years of Solitude*? Rhythm and blues? El Salvador? Rooted in the politics of the 1960s, *Multi-Cultural Literacy* might as well be called *Countercultural Literacy*. Among its contents is an essay by Paula Gunn Allen, "Who Is Your Mother? Red Roots of White Feminism," that offers an "Indian-focused version" of American history, designed to reaffirm the important place of women in the structure of tribal society; an essay by the black writer Ishmael Reed, "America: The Multinational Society," celebrating the "cultural bouillabaisse" of a nation where Yoruban, an African dialect, is spoken at a conference of Afro-American scholars in Milwaukee; and a list, modeled after Hirsch's, that includes Black Elk, Bo Diddley, Jack Kerouac, and Tonto (that's right, Tonto).

It's not only the literature syllabus that reflects this cultural counterinsurgency; the emphasis on minority cultures has pervaded the university. "What used to attract people to sociology is that we were able to look at blacks and Jews and Italians and see what is universal," says Egon Mayer, a professor of sociology at Brooklyn College. "Now those same students, who are Jews and blacks, want to study what's unique about themselves."

In history, which has gone the way of literature and sociology, there's even a term for it: "history from below." The

Federal Express has over 1,400 fully staffed Service Centers throughout the world—so there's always one close by, wherever you do business.

The Federal Express worldwide network provides on-time delivery of your documents, packages and freight in over 120 countries on six continents.

old history—elitist history, or "history from above"—studied kings, presidents, political leaders, and thinkers. The New History studies the anonymous masses: slaves, peasants, criminals, and the insane. Popular culture, the plight of women, the struggles of oppressed classes: these have now become the subject of legitimate inquiry for historians. "Mickey Mouse may in fact be more important to understanding the 1930s than Franklin Roosevelt," as one New Historian has put it; "the history of menarche is equal in importance to the history of monarchy," declares another.

The old-fashioned approach to literature and history, says Ishmael Reed, is a myth invented by Ivy League professors in order to impose their "small-screen view of political and cultural reality upon a complex world." Let's put behind us "the antebellum aesthetic position," says Henry Louis Gates Jr., the W. E. B. Du Bois Professor of Literature at Cornell and editor of *The Norton Anthology of Afro-American Literature*, decrying the days when "scholar-critics were white men and when women and people of other color were voiceless, faceless servants and laborers, pouring tea and filling brandy snifters in the boardrooms of old boys' clubs." Culture is a form of enslavement. The canon is just another racist scam.

In a way, this was what the debate at Stanford was about. "If you think we are talking about a handful of good books, you are mistaken," Bill King, a senior and president of the university's black-student union, declared in the spring of 1988, imploring the faculty senate to vote for a new curriculum. "We are discussing the foundations of education in America and the acceptance of Euro-America's place in the world as contributor, not creator." Why had he never been taught that Socrates, Herodotus, Pythagoras, and Solon owed much of what they knew to African cultures in Egypt, or that many of the words of Solomon were borrowed from the Egyptian writer Amenemope? Where, in the great scheme of things, were *his* people to be found?

To someone brought up on the idea that assimilation was an essential component of the American experience—that what established one's identity was the convergence, after several generations, of one's particular heritage and the generic

American traits of tolerance, openness, optimism, joy in opportunity—this insistence upon celebrating what could almost be described as a kind of ethnic tribalism is bewildering. Not even the socialists of the 1930s believed in secession from the republic; the revolution they hoped to bring about was a revolution of class, not race.

Yet "opening up the canon," as these efforts to expand the curriculum are called, isn't as radical as it seems. It's a populist, grass-roots phenomenon, American to the core. What could be more democratic than the new *Columbia Literary History of the United States* that incorporates Chippewa poems and Whitman's *Song of Myself*, Mark Twain and Jay McInerney? There are chapters on Afro-American literature, Mexican-American literature, Asian-American literature, on immigrant writers of the 19th century, and slave narratives of the Civil War.

"There isn't just one story of American literature," says Emory Elliott, a professor of English at the University of California at Riverside and the volume's general editor. "Things are wide open."

No group has been more assiduous in the effort to institutionalize new canonical discoveries than the feminists. Gynocriticism, the study of women's literature, has become a flourishing academic field. Catalogs list English-department courses entitled "Feminism, Modernism, and Postmodernism," "Shakespeare and Feminism," and "Feminist Theory and the Humanities." Margaret Williams Ferguson of Columbia University teaches a course on "Renaissance Women of Letters"—Christine de Pisan, Mary Sidney, Aphra Behn. "This is just the tip of the iceberg," says Harvard's Marjorie Garber. "These aren't just oddities or curiosities, but major writers."

The feminist enterprise is more than a matter of introducing works by women into the curriculum, or "mainstreaming." Men and women, it is now believed, have different responses to literature. What is needed, says Princeton's Elaine Showalter, is a "defamiliarization of masculinity, a poetics of the Other"—a critical methodology that addresses gender and sexual difference.

On campus bulletin boards I saw notices for lectures entitled "Coming Unstrung: Women, Men, Narrative, and Principles of Pleasure," "Men's Reading, Women's Writing: Canon-Formation and the Case of the 18th-Century French Novel," and "Abulia: Crises of Male Desire in Freud, Thomas Mann, and Musil."

For the post-'60s generation, lit crit is like child-rearing: both sexes share the burden. Lentricchia's work on Wallace Stevens attempts to sort out the poet's attitude toward his own masculinity—to "feminize" his image. At Harvard, Marjorie Garber is at work on a book about cross-dressing that discusses Peter Pan, Laurie Anderson, and old movies. "There's a lot of work to be done on cross-dressing," she says.

All these "texts" that are being rediscovered, republished, revalorized—the sermons and spinsters' diaries, the popular fiction of 1850: Are any of them masterpieces? Jane Tompkins makes a persuasive case for the merits of Susan Warner's *The Wide, Wide World* (reissued in 1986 by the Feminist Press), and it *is* a powerful book. The story of a young woman orphaned and exiled to bullying relatives in Scotland, Warner's novel portrays an experience of physical and spiritual renunciation that was obviously familiar to its 19th-century audience. The writing is energetic and vivid, and the humiliations endured by the heroine recall the trials of Lily Bart in Edith Wharton's *The House of Mirth* or Theodore Dreiser's *Sister Carrie*.

Only how do you know whether a book is good or not? Who decides and by what criteria? The discrimination of value that once occupied critics—that was, indeed, the business of critics from Dr. Johnson's *The Lives of the Poets* (1779-81) through the strenuously opinionated works of the British critic F. R. Leavis in the 1940s and 1950s—has become irrelevant. All that stuff that critics used to talk about, themes of love and death and heroism—forget it. There are no universals, Tompkins insists: "It is the context—which eventually includes the work itself—that creates the value its readers 'discover' there."

What the Duke critics discovered was "the historicization of value," says Stanley Fish. It's not that texts have no literal meaning, as the deconstructors who dominated literary studies in the 1970s believed; they have "an infinite plurality of meanings." The only way that we can hope to interpret a literary work is by knowing the vantage from which we perform the act of interpretation—in contemporary parlance, where we're coming from.

Barbara Herrnstein Smith, a power at Duke and a specialist in matters canonical, has written the definitive text on value relativity. *Contingencies of Value* is an exasperating book, especially the first chapter, where Smith clues us in about her life as a professor and claims to be so close to Shakespeare's sonnets that "there have been times when I believed that I had written them myself."

Still, for all her confessional posturing, her self-professed monstrous immodesty, Smith is on to something. What is taste? What do we experience when we contemplate a work of art? Like Fish, Smith is less interested in the status of a given work than in how that status is established. Who decides what's in and what's out? Those who possess "cultural power." What is art? Whatever the literary establishment says it is.

Smith's recent work is, among other things, a shrewd polemic against "high-culture critics" intent upon "epistemic self-stabilization" (that is to say, maintaining the status quo). What's wrong with high culture? It's elitist, hierarchical. The new vanguard, Smith asserts, is a tribe of "nonacculturated intellectuals," "postmodern cosmopolites," "exotic visitors and immigrants." In other words, professors.

The most innovative members of this new professoriate have transformed the landscape of contemporary literature. Many of them are tenured; they publish books. So why do they cultivate an image of themselves as literary outlaws? Frank Lentricchia isn't the only heavy academic dude around. D. A. Miller, a professor of comparative literature at Berkeley, has adorned his latest book with a photograph that mimes Lentricchia's notorious pose on the back of *Criticism and Social Change*—biceps rippling, arms folded across his chest like Mr. Clean.

Lentricchia's new book is entitled *Ariel and the Police*. Miller's is *The Novel and the Police*. Both are ostensibly works of literary criticism—Lentricchia is writing largely about William James and Michel Foucault; Miller, about the Victorian novel—but their real subject is the repressive nature of society, power and the containment of power, how our culture "polices" us.

"Where are the police in *Barchester Towers*?" Miller asks in a chapter on Trollope. Where, indeed? They're "literally nowhere to be found." No matter. Their very absence is significant, Miller claims, proof that Victorian England was a repressed society. The novel, then, is a form of concealment as well as of disclosure. Its truths are latent, murky, and undeclared. Miller's own aim as a critic is to "bring literature out of the classroom and into the closet."

What's going on here? Reading between the lines, one begins to get the message. The questioning of authority that's such a pervasive theme in criticism today is a theoretical version of battles that were fought on campuses 20 years ago—with real police. "The new epistemology—structuralism, deconstruction—provided the interpretive framework for challenging the canon," says Tompkins. "It's out in the hinterlands now. It's everywhere."

When you send your package Federal Express—domestic or
international—we take care of your shipment every step of the way.

THE DECLINE OF LITERARY CRITICISM

CHAPTER

5

Let us assume the worst: that innovations in the curriculum have politicized the humanities, that the proliferation of courses in third-world literature, of deconstructionism and feminist criticism, represents—I quote from Roger Kimball's new book, *Tenured Radicals: How Politics Has Corrupted Our Higher Education*—"an ideologically motivated assault on the intellectual and moral substance of our culture." That would be an unhappy development indeed. But even if there is a crisis in higher education, why is it a matter of public concern? So universities are going through a troubled phase: what impact does that have on the more immediate crisis—the deterioration of our inner-city schools?

It matters because values, conduct, and the prevailing moral tone are established at the top. What's taught at Erasmus Hall in Brooklyn or Jose de Diego Community Academy (formerly Tuley High School) on the West Side of Chicago reflects what's taught at City College of New York or Northwestern University. The revolution in the curriculum has already filtered down to the high schools.

For confirmation one need only consult a remarkable document entitled "A Curriculum of Inclusion." This 1989 report,

Thomas Sobol, the New York State commissioner of education, issued a report contending that textbooks teach minority groups to feel "alienated and devalued."

the product of a task force appointed by the New York State commissioner of education, Thomas Sobol, addressed the issue of how well the state's elementary and high school systems were responding to the needs of minority groups. Textbooks, the task force found, are dominated by a "Eurocentric conceptualization and modality" that emphasizes the dominance of whites. Members of minority cultures—African-Americans, Asian-Americans, Latinos, and Native Americans—learn from these textbooks to feel "alienated and devalued," while "members of the majority culture are exclusionary and overvalued." What the high school curriculum fails to teach, according to the Sobol report, is that the deck is stacked: our two-party system, the president's Cabinet, and Congress are "effective vehicles for articulating and aggregating the interests of the rich and powerful, the true benefactors of the 'new Anglo-Saxon model.'" The report's chief architect is Leonard Jeffries Jr., chairman of the Department of Black Studies at City College of New York.

The Sobol report elicited some harsh criticism. Diane Ravitch, a professor of history and education at Teachers College of Columbia University, noted that the 11th-grade syllabus described "the two major influences on the United States Constitution as the European Enlightenment and the political system of the Iroquois confederacy"—a unique interpretation of American history, to put it mildly. Like it or not, Andrew Hacker, a political scientist at Queens College, pointed out, "for almost all of this nation's history the major decisions have been made by white Christian men."

Maybe so, but the Sobol report was warmly received by the Board of Regents, which voted unanimously to adopt its findings. The drafting of a new curriculum for New York City public schools will soon be under way.

"A Curriculum of Inclusion" is hardly a singular phenomenon. The jargon of the canon-busters can also be found in the college boards, which now offer questions on child-rearing practices and the place of women in society. A sample: "How and why did the lives and status of Northern middle-class women change between 1776 and 1876?" It's not a bad question, actually; but how many 17-year-olds are prepared to answer it? Never mind. For the high school and college teachers who make up the exams, the important thing is to be *au courant*. The Committee of Examiners in Advanced Placement (AP) American History "believed the AP program should be on the cutting edge of curricular reform," reports the historian Gertrude Himmelfarb, "and this view eventually prevailed."

The New History, like the new literary criticism, is no mere fad, Himmelfarb makes clear; it's closer to "a revolution in the discipline." And the consequences of this revolution are widely felt. What's taught in graduate school will eventually be taught in college and high school. Higher education sets the national agenda. "The examinations send out signals to high schools throughout the country telling

Hilton Kramer, editor of *The New Criterion*, says the universities, once bastions of high culture, now dabble in "the trash of popular culture"—a development that puts our civilization in jeopardy.

them what kind of history should be taught if their students are to compete successfully for admission to college," writes Himmelfarb; in effect, they "establish something very like a national curriculum."

How are the universities fulfilling that function? In attempting to make students skeptical about the current consensus, have they gone too far? For an older generation of professors, the transformation of their genteel profession into a battleground of gender, class, and ideology has been a disaster. The teaching of literature, objects R.W.B. Lewis, the biographer of Edith Wharton and a former professor of English at Yale, is "politics with the history left out and, indeed, politics with the literature left out." But of course it's not just politics that Lewis and his venerable colleagues abhor; it's the *kind* of politics. From their perspective, opening up the canon is nothing less than an intellectual counterinsurgency movement—a cover for smuggling into the classroom the countercultural agenda of the 1960s. Once bastions of high culture, the universities now dabble in what Hilton Kramer, editor of the neo-conservative journal *The New Criterion*, refers to as "the trash of popular culture."

All this talk of expanding the curriculum, allowing new voices to be heard and acknowledging the importance of other cultures in the shaping of our own, is really an excuse for laissez-faire education, say the traditionalists—the curricular version of "do your own thing." Make no mistake about it, warns Kramer: the politicization of literary studies, the blurring of distinctions between pop culture and high culture, is no mere squabble among professors. "It is our civilization that we believe to be at stake in this struggle," Kramer declared in a recent issue of *The New Criterion*. "The defense of art must not, in other words, be looked upon as a luxury of civilization—to be indulged in and supported when all else is serene and unchallenged—but as the very essence of our civilization."

Politics—the advocacy of a specific ideological cause—is, and always has been, the enemy of art. In the 1930s, the demand for Socialist Realism in Russia—explicit depiction of the class struggle, "correct" art—silenced a whole generation of Soviet writers. Bureaucrats in the Writers' Union determined what got published, while geniuses like Osip Mandelstam, who made the mistake of writing a satirical poem about Stalin, perished in Siberian labor camps. Kramer sees the same thing happening now: a cadre of professors, academic *apparatchiks*, has once again appropriated the humanities for its own ideological purposes. The proliferation of ethnic, racial, and gender studies represents nothing less than "the transformation of art into social science." Ignoring the work of art as *art*, scholars concentrate exclusively on the political and economic conditions that produced it. To reduce art to such narrow preoccupations, Kramer insists, is to deny the transcendent, universal values that give it meaning—to install in the domain of imagination a totalitarian regime:

> So advanced and widespread is this surrender of the
> arts and the humanities to the social sciences—and to
> the radical political agenda of the social sciences—that
> we now have reason, I believe, to look upon the social
> sciences as a kind of academic gulag to which, on one
> campus after another and in one learned journal after
> another, the arts and the sciences have been sent for
> what, in other parts of the world, it is customary to
> describe as "reeducation" or "rehabilitation"—in
> other words, brainwashing.

The rhetoric may be exaggerated, but the situation is much as Kramer describes it. The radicalization of the humanities is an accomplished fact. The new five-volume Cambridge *New History of American Literature*, edited by Sacvan Bercovitch, a professor of English and American literature at Harvard, provides clear evidence of this development. Professor Bercovitch's contributors aren't members of the old guard, he explained in a preliminary essay describing the project, but "Americans trained in the '60s and early '70s, spokespersons for 'dissensus.'" For the New Americanists, as the critic Frederick Crews has labeled this generation of scholars, it's not only the curriculum that is undergoing renovation, not only the way books are read. "The New Americanist program," writes Crews, "aims at altering the literary departments' social makeup as well their dominant style of criticism."

In the last decade, the progenitors of English studies have produced a whole new critical vocabulary. After the politics of gender, the "feminization" of literature, and the assault on the canon, English departments have moved on to "social constructionism," which teaches that literature can be understood only in terms of power—who had it and who didn't. Mark Twain, for instance, is no longer seen as the wise, acerbic humorist revered by generations of readers, according to the Twain scholar Susan Gillman, but as "a deeply historicized writer" whose "most apparently unique and idiosyncratic representations of problematic identity engage with late-19th-century efforts to classify human behavior within biological, sexual, racial, and psychological parameters." Twain's books, however idiosyncratic their points of view, say the scholars, offer clues to the power relationships that defined 19th-century America. He was, despite himself, a representative man.

This trend toward "historicizing" and "ideologizing" works of literature has become institutionalized in our universities. One need only glance over the 1988-89 reading list for one of Stanford's new "Culture, Ideas, Values" survey courses to see which way the wind is blowing. There, among a few survivors from the precanonical era—the Bible, Aeschylus, and Shakespeare—one finds *With His Pistol in His Hand* by Americo Paredes, *He Who Does Evil Should Expect No Good* by Juana Manuela Gorritti, and something called "Documents From the Tupac Amani Rebellion." The presence of such a reading list on a campus known for its conservative approach to the humanities makes it hard to dismiss as paranoia Hilton Kramer's contention that universities are now firmly in the hands of the radical left.

In itself, the politicization of the university is hardly a new phenomenon. The era from 1945 to 1960, generally thought to have been so quiescent—the Eisenhower years, the tranquilized '50s—was in fact "a period of constantly growing political commitment, political zeal, and political ideology," wrote Robert Nisbet in his classic book about American education in the postwar era, *The Degradation of the Academic Dogma*. The hostile attention that Senator Joseph McCarthy trained on communists, real and imagined, in the universities during the 1950s served to radicalize them in self-defense.

What distinguishes academic politics now from academic politics then? Politicization—I reluctantly employ these unwieldy words—has been accompanied by professionalization. The ex-radicals in college English departments aren't motivated to write the way they do out of a determination to overthrow the United States government; it's become the approved way of finding something new to say about old books. In 1987, according to *The New York Times* education reporter Edward B. Fiske, scholarly journals published 215 articles on Milton, 132 on Henry James, and 554 on Shakespeare. How can an associate professor, up for tenure, find anything new to say about these authors? It isn't easy. Thus the trend described by Northwestern professor Lawrence Lipking as "competitive reading"—the quest for innovative interpretations, for "the reading that curves or swerves, like a grading curve," as Lipking put it not long ago in *The New Republic*. "The further the student advances, the more curves are needed, until finally, in graduate school, the choice of reading differs so much from the texts most other people have read, or the interpretation differs so much from earlier interpretations, that it becomes publishable."

I offer, in support of Professor Lipking's thesis, a recent essay published in the *Yale Journal of Criticism* entitled "Auto-canonization: Tropes of Self-Legitimation in 'Popular Culture.'" This essay, by Jonathan Freedman, a professor of English at Yale, examines the implications of opening up the canon, and what might happen if it was really opened up. Interpreting, in the approved deconstructionist fashion, a song by Barry Manilow entitled "I Write the Songs," Professor Freedman discovers that the "I" of the song is a highly problematic figure whose identity depends on two crucial assumptions:

> . . . first, that the songs are written not in the Derridean sense of the written as the arbitrary or the impersonal but rather in the older sense of the written as composed, as organized by a primary, fully individuated consciousness exercising itself in acts of sponta-

neous but disciplined creativity; and second, that this consciousness, this "I" that writes the songs, has some sort of social role or function to fulfill in the world at large.

Let me offer another sample, one that reflects a somewhat different but still characteristic methodology. I choose, virtually at random, a sentence from *The Critical Difference: Essays in the Contemporary Rhetoric of Reading* by Barbara Johnson: "In his median position between the Budd/Claggart opposition and the acceptance/irony opposition, Captain Vere functions as a focus for the conversion of polarity into ambiguity and back again." The discussion is of Melville's *Billy Budd*; the author teaches in the departments of French and comparative literature at Harvard. As a sentence, it's no better or worse than many thousands like it, and it's certainly no more obscure; to someone trained in the language of contemporary criticism, it does indeed yield a meaning. Captain Vere is a *reader*, stresses Professor Johnson; which isn't to say that he reads books, but rather that he is the character whose interpretations of motive and character are said to represent Melville's own. But of course we can't ascribe a particular interpretation to Vere/Melville's "reading" of events; interpretation, remember, is an activity fraught with variables. The "reader's" point of view is inherently unstable; to criticize a work of art is to assess our ignorance—in effect, to question the whole enterprise.

Does criticism have to be written this way? There are plenty of critics around—especially critics of an older generation— who are willing to put their readings on the line. The eminent Harold Bloom of Yale, for one—however intricate his own critical vocabulary—has never been shy about saying what a poem or novel means. But the critical method practiced by Freedman and Johnson dominates the scene, and it has a trickle-down effect. When students do read, complains William Pritchard, a professor of English at Amherst and one of the few critics around who writes for a general audience, they're more likely to have read the French deconstructionist Jacques Derrida on Rousseau or Roland Barthes on Balzac than Rousseau or Balzac. They become adept at a kind of

Every business day, Federal Express delivers over 14 million pounds of documents, packages and freight throughout the world.

Our international delivery experts can answer your questions,
24 hours a day, 365 days a year.

academic discourse learned from their professors, who spend their time discussing "what XY recently wrote about *Jane Eyre* in the last issue of *Diacritics* or *Signs*."

This is how it's done now. The civilizing purpose of literature, its capacity to inculcate values even as it teaches us about the ambiguity of human conduct, is a thing of the past. "The best citizen," claimed Lionel Trilling, "is the person who has learned from the great minds and souls of the past how beautiful reason and virtue are and how difficult to attain." How archaic those words sound now! They reflect a humility that's vanished from the scene. The critic is the artist now. The way to be original is to come up with an interpretation that appropriates the literary text to the critic's design. As a disenchanted professor quoted in Lynne Cheney's report puts it, "The level of specialization increases, while the significance of research moves toward the vanishing point."

Edmund Wilson said the Modern Language Association's seminars were meant to serve as "self-qualifications in what is really an employment agency."

Attacks on academic pedantry are nothing new. The late Edmund Wilson, in his famous attack on the Modern Language Association and its methods, "The Fruits of the MLA," produced a masterpiece of satirical muckraking. Perusing the program of the association's 1968 convention, Wilson was greatly amused by the announced topics, among them "Flowers, Women, and Song in the Poetry of William Carlos Williams" and "The Unity of George Peele's *The Old Wives' Tale*"—topics that seem straightforward compared with the elaborate titles of today. Of course, these seminars weren't meant to appeal to a general audience, Wilson concluded, "but to serve as offered self-qualifications in what is really an employment agency" (same as now). As for the "definitive editions" that so many MLA scholars labored over, huge volumes laden with textual commentary about variant spellings and other equally weighty matters, Wilson marveled at the sheer expenditure of energy: texts were submitted to the scrutiny of a device known as the Hinman Collating Machine, which registered discrepancies in drafts; they were read backward by professional proofreaders in order to discover typos without being distracted by the words' sense. Apropos the official edition of Melville's

Typee, Wilson reported, quoting from its preface: "And then there is the great hyphenation problem: 'The missing hyphen in *married* at E213-2 (191.34) is also obvious, since the word is not a compound.'"

Things were no better when I attended the MLA's 1986 convention. The program was equally bewildering: hundreds upon hundreds of conferences devoted to such special themes as "Eddie and May's Old Man: Theatricality in Sam Shepard's *Fool for Love*," "Hannah Cooks the Turkey: Woody Allen's Accommodations of Postmodern Irony," "The Repressions of Psychoanalysis: Lesbians, Mothers, and Others in Literature and Theory," and many, many more. Literature wasn't the only subject on the agenda: attention was also paid to the so-called real world. You could attend workshops on the travails of part-time teaching ("Out of the Bus and Into the Bullpen: The Adjunct Life at Queens"), on "The Impact of Homo- and Lesbophobia on Academic Careers," on "Pragmatic Dissonance in Greeting-Card Humor," on "*Bright Lights, Big City*, Back to the 'Burbs: Jay McInerney's Encounter With the Other." One of my journalistic colleagues on the MLA beat described this literary Balkanization as "breaking down constituencies by gender and body size." (Sure enough, there was a session entitled "Seizing Power: Gender, Representation, and Body Scale.")

As a rule, I'm suspicious of literary journalists who put down professors. I suspect them of the ambivalence I feel myself—a mixture of envy toward the pastoral surroundings in which they work and contempt for their unworldliness. But scholars themselves are more than willing to testify about the decline of purposeful scholarship within their ranks. "To anyone who pays attention to current controversies," writes Lawrence Lipking of Northwestern, referring to the curriculum issue, "nothing could be plainer than that most of the disputants have not read the works that the others are proposing." His colleague Gerald Graff, who has been urging that the debate itself ought to become part of the universities' curriculum, is even blunter: "At the very moment when external forces have conspired to deflate the importance and truth of literature, literary theory delivers the final blow itself." Or consider this remarkable bit of testimony:

> English and literary studies have reached a point in
> their theoretical development when they've become
> almost incapable of communicating to the layman at
> the very historical moment when they've most
> needed to justify their existence. The brightest and
> most innovative people in literary criticism are as
> impenetrable as nuclear physicists. The left-wing in-
> telligentsia is trapped in a kind of ghetto that only they
> understand, and so can't bring any leverage to bear on
> the body politic.

The writer is David Lodge, a well-known English novelist
and, until a few years ago, a professor of modern English
literature at the University of Birmingham. (He is also the
editor of a collection of essays on deconstructionism.) The
situation he deplores in England is virtually identical to
the situation here.

Academics have been notably reticent in the face of all this
criticism. The only significant rebuttal I know of is a pamphlet
issued by the American Council of Learned Societies (ACLS),
an association of scholars and scholarly groups. Instigated as a
response to Lynne Cheney's attack on the universities, ACLS
Occasional Paper No. 7 constitutes a reply of sorts to the
charges leveled against English professors and their kind—a
defense of academic theory and practice. Entitled "Speaking
for the Humanities," No. 7 is a collaborative enterprise—the
pamphlet is signed by six professors whose efforts were co-
ordinated by Professor George Levine of Rutgers University.
Their intent is to answer attacks on the humanities that have
lately called attention to the state of learning in the universities, "for those attacks have practical consequences that will
affect the future development, not only of the humanities, but
of society as well."

Canon-busting is in the ascendant, contend the authors of
"Speaking for the Humanities," so there must be something
to it: "Much of what most matters in modern thought challenges claims to universality and subverts traditional assumptions of authority." And since it's in the ascendant, the New
Canonists—to coin a term—are merely doing their duty. The

specialization that Cheney deplored is the result of attempts to be "professionals rather than amateurs—belletrists who un-self-consciously sustain traditional hierarchies, traditional so-cial and cultural exclusions, assuming that their audience is both universal and homogenous." I translate: Those who endorse a core curriculum, a canon of great works, are old-fashioned. To claim that such a canon exists is to discriminate against the literature of minorities. To teach this canon is to ignore the ethnic diversity of college students in the 1990s. Specialization is a necessary aspect of *professionalization*; it enables professors to develop alternative canons, to challenge the status quo. According to the authors of ACLS Paper No. 7, that is a good thing: "For professionalization makes thought possible by developing sets of questions, imposing norms which have then to be questioned and thereby promoting debate on key problems." *Professionalization makes thought possible*. As Gertrude Stein once said, "Interesting if true."

Is the situation really so dire? In fact, contend the authors of ACLS Occasional Paper No. 7, what we are witnessing is a revival of the humanities. The statistics trotted out by bureau-crats like Bennett and Cheney are inconclusive, they assert; in many universities, the number of students enrolled in English and history majors is up. They point approvingly to "the proliferation of interdisciplinary humanities centers" dedi-cated to the promotion of learning in a wide variety of fields, from philosophy to psychoanalysis. If the humanities *are* in trouble, they stress, it's not entirely the humanists' fault. There has always been a virulent strain of philistinism in American life. Cheney's broadside is merely the latest symp-tom of it:

> United States society, with a tradition of anti-intellec-tualism and interest in science, engineering, eco-nomics, has been finding it convenient to indict the humanities for their intellectual weaknesses in at-tempting to engage practical moral and social issues; they have, so the charge goes, lapsed from the Ar-noldian ideals of seeing the object as it really is and learning the best that has been thought and said. Instead, they allegedly pander to new interest groups

> and mix the universal ideals of art and morality with
> history, politics, gender, and race. Thus, alarming
> changes that are surely primarily connected to na-
> tional and international restructuring of political and
> economic power are partly attributed to the failure of
> the humanities to think unmixedly and speak un-
> equivocally for the universal values in the Western
> traditions of art, literature, and philosophy.

This is supposed to be an ironic summation of the conservative point of view, but it's actually a succinct indictment of the
case against the New Canonists.

How does this "restructuring of political and economic
power" affect the humanities? George Levine, chief editor of
the ACLS paper, has an explanation: "While campus interest
in the humanities declined, the United States began to doubt
that it was still the leading economic power of the world," he
wrote in a recent issue of *Raritan*, a quarterly journal associ-
ated with Rutgers University. "At the same time, middle-class
students began to wonder if they could expect to achieve the
economic status of their own parents." In other words, the
humanities are a luxury to be dispensed with in belt-tighten-
ing times. Students are no longer willing to make the sacri-
fices necessary for a career in higher learning. If becoming an
English professor means forfeiting our inalienable right to a
two-car garage, forget it.

Whether the oil crisis of 1973 will prove to have been
partially responsible for the declining enrollment in the humanities, as Professor Levine maintains, is a highly debatable
proposition. One could just as easily argue that the arts and
humanities prosper in unprosperous times, that economic
recessions promote the kind of holiday from materialistic
ambition that memoirists of the 1930s and 1940s remember so
fondly. For many writers and intellectuals, the Depression
was a liberating time, a time of freedom. "No longer chained
to the wheel of career and profession," the philosopher
William Barrett recalled in his memoir, *The Truants*, "we
could abandon ourselves to the delight of irrelevant studies."
You might as well be a graduate student if you couldn't get a
job.

Those days, of course, are long gone. Barrett's vision of the good life—idling away afternoons on a bench in Washington Square with the latest issue of *Partisan Review*—is archaic, quaint. Ours is an increasingly nonverbal culture, a culture in which books no longer possess the aura of sanctity they once did. The undergraduates of this generation were brought up on television. They weren't brought up to read. The ecstatic literary apprenticeship that Alfred Kazin, our foremost critic, so rapturously evoked in his classic memoir, *A Walker in the City*, of entering the Brownsville Public Library on a summer's evening and "trembling in front of the shelves," isn't an experience likely to find its way into the memoirs of my generation. Reminiscing in *The New Republic*'s 75th-anniversary issue about his career as a man of letters, Kazin supplied a memorable epitaph: "Our literary period may yet be remembered as one in which the book business replaced the literary world, in which literary theory replaced literature, and in which, as Irving Howe has said, Marxism came to its end—in the English Department."

The 1960s aren't wholly to blame. The idea of the university as a place where disinterested scholarship could flourish was threatened long before the attack on the canon. Its demise can be dated back to the postwar era. Until then, the universities' mandate was assumed—"that it is good for students to read Chaucer, Jane Austen, T. S. Eliot, good to study history, philosophy, sociology, and physics, good to accumulate knowledge in the learned disciplines, each of these good in and for itself," as Robert Nisbet put it in *The Degradation of the Academic Dogma*. In the 1940s, a new phenomenon was visited upon the academic community—what Nisbet variously calls "the higher capitalism," "the new capitalism," and "academic capitalism." The universities were invaded by government and private foundations. Suddenly the big money was in research. Institutes, centers, and bureaus sprang up on campuses across the land. "For the first time in Western history, professors and scholars were thrust into the unwonted position of entrepreneurs in incessant search for new sources of capital, of new revenue, and, taking the word in its larger sense, of profits." Universities became bureaucratic institutions. Professors became captains of intellectual industry. The humanities became irrelevant.

As long as the *idea* of learning was respected, the humanists could survive and go about their work of education. The acquisition of general culture was still regarded as a virtue, if not a necessity. But it turns out that culture is a myth, according to the professoriate, a tool for establishing hierarchies of value; in effect, culture is an instrument of oppression. Given the prevalence of this attitude, it's not only unreasonable to demand that students master a core of classics, it's hypocritical. Their professors haven't mastered it. Their professors don't even believe in it. Why should they?

To expedite the on-time delivery of your international shipments, Federal Express has Customs agents on site in the U.S. and at many of our overseas hubs.

THE END
OF
TRADITION

In his classic memoir, *Enemies of Promise*, the late critic Cyril Connolly invokes the litany of English writers he absorbed as a boy at Eton: "Webster was my favorite Elizabethan, then came Donne, and after him Marvell, Herrick, and Sir Thomas Browne." Connolly read Boswell, Gibbon, and Laurence Sterne; he wallowed in the Romantic poets. It was an education typical of that day and class—it's still typical today. To be literate in England is to be thoroughly acquainted with its literature. The classics of English prose and poetry resonate in the popular imagination. London newspaper columnists quote Macaulay. Politicians and government officials write scholarly books. Noel Annan, the former minister of education, is an authority on the literature of Victorian England. Michael Foot, once head of the Labor Party, has published a creditable biography of Byron.

For England's middle and upper classes, literature is part of their cultural inheritance. It reflects their customs, their speech, their experience of the world—a world that in some crucial respects hasn't changed for centuries. The London of Thackeray, the London of Dickens, isn't all that different from the London of Kingsley (or even Martin) Amis, the celebrated father-and-son team of contemporary British fiction. There is continuity.

The same could be said of France, where writers are public figures, even heroes, and always have been. André Malraux, de Gaulle's minister of culture, was a major novelist. Twenty-five thousand people attended the funeral of Jean-Paul Sartre. The French Academy, composed of 40 eminent *hommes de lettres*, is a more august body than its senate. Every *lycéen* knows his way around the Pléiade editions, those handsome, beautifully produced volumes of the French classics printed on thin paper. The national literature and the national identity are one.

Englishness and Frenchness are complex traits, not easily susceptible to definition. They embrace profound differences of class, accent, and background. But they compose recognizable identities all the same; they describe a national type. There is a certain insularity about these cultures; even so, it's hard for an American not to envy their cozy self-regard. I remember once, walking in the countryside of Cornwall with an English poet who amazed me with his knowledge of local lore. Each stone, each house, each ancient church had its history. Kings had trod this ground.

It's exhausting to be an American—you have to conjure up an identity out of nothing, become self-made. Character is fate. In England, character is also fate, but so is heredity; the visible evidence of tradition enables English citizens to think of themselves as transitory tenants of a nation that is destined to outlast them.

Americans are immigrants. We're all from somewhere else. After the Puritans and other dissenting sects came the Scandinavians, the Swiss, the Irish, the Jews of Eastern Europe, the Italians, the Chinese. Since World War II, our borders have been overwhelmed by new hyphenated populations: Asian-Americans, Mexican-Americans, Russian-Americans. Flatbush Avenue in Brooklyn has been colonized by Ethiopians, Trinidadians, Tibetans, and Pakistanis. They're citizens of the United States. Americans? There is no such indigenous type.

Yet we have an American literature. The great 19th-century flowering that produced Whitman, Hawthorne, Melville, Emerson, and Thoreau—main figures of what came to be known as the American Renaissance—was evidence that we possessed, if not a national identity, at the very least a culture of our own. "When one looks back at Victorian England and the America of Whitman and Lincoln," writes David Bromwich of Yale in his essay "The Future of Tradition: Notes on the Crisis in the Humanities," "one is impressed by the consensus a majority of the educated observed in the arts and moral sciences. Not, indeed, a consensus of judgment, but a consensus about the grounds of judgment." In politics and sensibility this majority was progressive, liberal, and egalitarian; it was attuned to "the topics of the time," wrote Emerson: "the literature of the poor, the feelings of the child, the philosophy of the street, the meaning of a household life." It shared a set of assumptions and beliefs that, in their aggregate, could be called American.

Our literature, like our political tradition, is essentially democratic. The great American novelists of the period between the two world wars—Hemingway and Fitzgerald, Faulkner and Thomas Wolfe—came out of the provinces to produce a distinctive American idiom. Like their 19th-century predecessors, they were radically unalike: their books are a compendium of the American vernacular, from the laconic Midwestern idiom of Hemingway's Nick Adams stories to the sophisticated New York slang of F. Scott Fitzgerald, from the backwoods South of Faulkner to the North Carolina mountain dialect of Wolfe. Yet they had studied—and were determined to emulate—the masters of English literature. Faulkner started out as a poet, writing bad Elizabethan verse. Thomas Wolfe was inspired by the King James Bible.

The novelists of the postwar generation apprenticed themselves to the same literary tradition. English poets like Milton and Coleridge were far from the experience of a Jewish writer like Saul Bellow when he was growing up on the West Side of Chicago in a Yiddish-speaking home; they might as well have been writing in a foreign language. All the same, these were the authors he read in school. Bellow has a wonderful image in one of his unpublished memoirs of an old Swedish schoolteacher reciting *King Lear* to a roomful of Jewish children whose parents were just off the boat. "I did not go to the public library to read the Talmud," he notes in *Starting Out in Chicago*, "but the novels and poems of Sherwood Anderson, Theodore Dreiser, Edgar Lee Masters, and Vachel Lindsay." They had interpreted the New World, had made it real: "These were people who had resisted the material weight of American society and who proved—what was not immediately obvious—that the life lived in great manufacturing, shipping, and banking centers, with their slaughter stink, their great slums, prisons, hospitals, and schools, was also a human life."

There *was* an America, then—the America that was in these books. And it was the children of immigrants—writers like Irving Howe, Lionel Trilling, and Philip Rahv—who would turn out to be among the most articulate interpreters of English and American literature in the postwar era. Trilling on Hawthorne, Howe on Sherwood Anderson, Rahv on Henry James (a writer whose place in the canon he was instrumental in restoring): these writers knew their way around the Europeans, but it was their own native literature, the literature of their new America, that excited their imaginations.

And their politics? In their own way, these critics were radicals long before university English departments became Marxist cells. Howe has been a socialist all his life; Rahv was a founder of the left-wing *Partisan Review*; Trilling was a critic of liberalism who remained a liberal all his life. But they didn't consider it their job to lobby for opening up the canon; they weren't in the business of getting Jewish writers like Sholem Aleichem and Isaac Babel on the syllabus. Some books you read on your own.

Nor were they Anglophiles (even if some of them affected an English manner). What primarily appealed to them about the classics of English and American literature that they taught and interpreted with such spontaneous ardor was that it was somehow *theirs*. To read Whitman's *Democratic Vistas* or Henry James's *The American Scene* (even if it did contain some brutal antisemitic passages) was to be infused with a spontaneous vitality, a sense of belonging to the New World in which they'd only just arrived. No one has written more eloquently about the tremendous impact of this literature than Alfred Kazin. "The past, the past was great," he exulted in *A Walker in the City*. "I read as if books would fill my every gap, legitimize my strange quest for the American past, remedy my every flaw, let me in at last into the great world that was anything just out of Brownsville." To know, to possess and claim that past as one's own, was to become American.

Jews weren't the only ones eager to celebrate what they regarded as *their* literature. As other minorities made their way up and seized the opportunities for higher education that became available to them, they responded in the same way. As a boy, Henry Louis Gates Jr., now a leading scholar in the field of Afro-American studies, copied out passages from Charles Dickens and Jane Austen, passages that named what he "deeply felt but could not say." The black writer Maya Angelou, called upon as a child to recite a poem before her church congregation in Stamps, Arkansas, chose Portia's speech from *The Merchant of Venice*. "Nobody else understands it," she recalled, "but I *know* that William Shakespeare was a black woman. That is the role of art in life." We identify with the great characters in fiction because we recognize our own experience of the world in theirs—not because of the color of their skin.

If you're a black woman these days, you're more likely to read a book that was written by one: a Toni Morrison novel; a slave diary resurrected from some newly exhumed Civil War archive; a memoir by Maya Angelou. In the new curricular scheme of things, the books that used to be considered classics aren't as universal as we thought they were. The canon of English and American literature turns out to be a conspiracy of the dominant class. In *Sensational Designs*, Jane Tompkins quotes a famous passage in F. O. Matthiessen's *American Renaissance* in which he singles out for praise the half-decade 1850-55, which produced (among other books) Emerson's *Representative Men*, Hawthorne's *The Scarlet Letter*, Melville's *Moby Dick*, and Whitman's *Leaves of Grass*. This list, Tompkins objects, set the agenda for generations of undergraduates. What's wrong with it? It's "exclusive and class-bound," it "embodies the views of a very small, socially, culturally, geographically, sexually, and racially restricted elite." There are no works by women on Matthiessen's list; no works that deal with "the issues of abolition and temperance" that dominated the national consciousness in those days; "no works by males not of Anglo-Saxon origin; and, indeed, no works by writers living south of New York, north of Boston, or west of Stockbridge, Massachusetts." So much for a reading list that purports to depict the whole soul of man.

For Tompkins, the old order is a WASP enclave, the literary

equivalent of the Metropolitan Club. Just the opposite, proponents of this old order respond. "It used to be thought that ideas transcended race, gender, and class," Gertrude Himmelfarb writes wistfully on the op-ed page of *The New York Times*, "that there are such things as truth, reason, morality, and artistic excellence, which can be understood and aspired to by everyone, of whatever race, gender, or class." Great literature is literature with a universal message. Its purpose, says Walter Jackson Bate, is to instruct us in "the whole experience of life."

Only what is this *whole*? The right is just as "exclusionist" as the left when it comes to defining it. The best that has been thought and said is actually the best that has been thought and said by a tiny elite. "The real community of man," Allan Bloom asserts, "is the community of those who seek the truth, of the potential knowers, that is, in principle, of all men to the extent they desire to know." He doesn't mean "all men," of course. If he did, there wouldn't have been so many objections to his book. The culture that he values is the culture of the West. Bloom clings to the idea that Socrates, Plato, Machiavelli, Rousseau, Kant, and a handful of others constitute a precious legacy; they represent the culture we've inherited. And some cultures happen to be—in Orwell's famous phrase—more equal than others. Ours is one of them. As Bloom's colleague Saul Bellow so memorably put it, "Who is the Tolstoy of the Zulus? The Proust of the Papuans? I'd be glad to read him."

Bloom's message is outwardly patriotic: "The United States is one of the highest and most extreme achievements of the rational quest for the good life according to nature." But a close reading of his book makes it clear that Bloom isn't interested in our culture, except in the broadest sense—our culture as it derives from antiquity and the European nation-states whose achievements were built upon it, the culture whose artifacts are to be found in every museum and church in Europe. Too often, the debate over Western civilization fails to examine what anyone means by Western civilization. For Bloom and his ideological compatriots, Western civ

stands for something more than Plato and Aristotle, the Great
Books, the best that has been thought and said. It's a synonym
for high culture, the kind of high culture *they* soaked up when
they were students. "The longing for Europe has been all but
extinguished in the young," mourns Bloom. Youth worships
at a different shrine now. The grand tour isn't what it was in
Henry James's day, a pilgrimage to the citadels of art in Rome
and Venice, Paris and London—the civilization that nour-
ished James and George Santayana. The young still go abroad
on their summer vacations, flying Virgin Atlantic with Harvard *Let's Go* guides in their backpacks; but Europe as a theater
of self-improvement is obsolete.

It's interesting that Bloom scarcely discusses American literature in his book. The transcendentalists and their literary
heirs play no part in his scheme of things. As Arthur
Schlesinger Jr. has pointed out in a brilliant essay entitled
"The Opening of the American Mind," Bloom "spends 400
pages laying down the law about the American mind and
never once mentions the two greatest and most characteristic
American thinkers, Emerson and William James." Why?
Schlesinger conjectures: "It is because he would have had to
concede the fact that the American mind is by nature and
tradition skeptical, irreverent, pluralistic, and relativistic."

Bloom would admit to the charge. Only for him, these
traits are double-edged. Tolerance is no virtue; it's a license to
dilute the purity of our high cultural inheritance with infu-
sions from the crude materialistic culture that America represents. What's good about America—or what used to be
good—isn't to be found on the American-literature shelf.
What's good about America is our capacity for freedom, says
Bloom—freedom to reason, to discriminate, to decide for
oneself what is just and right. How do we acquire this capacity? By reading the Great Books.

But freedom, like the whole soul of man, is hard to define.
Both sides in the book wars have appropriated it. Both sides
maintain that the goal of education is realizing one's true self.
This sounds good, but what does it mean? As I understand it,
the discovery of self is achieved through the exercise of skep-
ticism, challenging the status quo, learning independence of

mind. To cultivate the faculty of reason is to discover one's true nature. To know oneself is to fulfill Bloom's definition of the philosopher's mandate—"to know things as they are."

How can we achieve that goal? The philosopher Richard Rorty, a self-professed disciple of the great American pragmatist and educator John Dewey, offers a very Deweyan solution: in order to "realize" themselves, the young must know their own history. The Revolutionary War, the Civil War, the women's suffrage movement, abolition—these events constitute, in Rorty's words, a "narrative of freedom and hope." They provide a lesson in moral conduct and values. "The point of non-vocational higher education is to help students realize that they can reshape themselves," argues Rorty, "that they can rework the self-image foisted on them by their past, the self-image that makes them competent citizens, into a new self-image, one that they themselves have helped to create."

Yes, but whose self-image? Isn't even the narrative Rorty envisions "privileged"—that is to say, the creation of an educational establishment? What we choose to read determines how we interpret our collective past. The purportedly neglected classics that Jane Tompkins recommends—*Uncle Tom's Cabin*, Susan Warner's *The Wide, Wide World*, the novels of Brockden Brown—aren't simply her personal best; they're propaganda weapons in a war. "The literary canon, as codified by a cultural elite, has power to influence the way the country thinks across a broad range of issues," Tompkins concludes. "The struggle now being waged in the professoriate over which writers deserve canonical status is not just a struggle over the relative merits of literary geniuses; it is a struggle among contending factions for the right to be represented in the picture America draws of itself."

Where are the women? Where are the Indians? Where are the slaves? We can't just paint them out. And even if we acknowledge them, even if we agree that our own history is the one we ought to study first, whose version is it, anyway? After all, insist the New Americanists, we must beware of what Frederick Crews describes (not without irony) as "literary nationalism"—the optimistic notion of progress inscribed

Federal Express has over 14,000 couriers overseas, providing on-time delivery of your international documents, packages and freight virtually anywhere in the world.

Put the power of the Federal Express shipping management system at your fingertips. With the Powership 2® you can eliminate paperwork and the reconciliation of invoices, and even track packages on-line.

in traditional approaches to American literature and history. "America" is a myth like any other. Behind the stories our children learn in school—the Boston Tea Party, the Emancipation Proclamation, the uplifting sagas of a people determined to be free—lurk other, darker themes: racism, class struggle, the suppression of "marginalized" groups. The canon of American literature put forward by F. O. Matthiessen ignores these constituencies, say Tompkins and her comrades on the literary barricades. Its claim to universality is spurious.

Sidney Hook, in a shrewd article entitled "The Closing of the American Mind: An Intellectual Best-Seller Revisited"—the last thing he wrote before his recent death at the age of 86—supplied a persuasive rebuttal to this argument. A partisan of no party, Hook was a conservative who had been a Marxist in his youth. His conservatism was tempered by a sympathy for the egalitarian impulses of the left if not for its grasp of logic. "Of course the culture of the past was created by the elite members of the past!" Hook exclaimed. "Who else could have created it at a time when literacy itself was the monopoly of the elite classes?"

The late Sidney Hook pointed out that the books under attack by the left were themselves profoundly radical.

What no one until Hook had bothered to point out was that the very works now under attack as elitist were themselves profoundly radical. Rousseau's *Confessions*, Milton's *Areopagitica*, and Thoreau's *Walden* were among the most eloquent critiques of established authority ever produced. And even revolutionary thinkers were known to admire the classics of those cultures whose politics they deplored. Marx himself, Hook reminds us, conceded that while Greek art and culture were the products of a class society, "they still prevail as the standard and model beyond attainment."

Hook also disposed of the notion that undergraduates should study their own racial and ethnic literature. Art is supposed to hold a mirror up to nature, not to the artist. "Does one have to be French to study or understand Napoleon, Russian to understand Lenin, Greek to read Homer or enjoy the figures of Praxiteles?" asked Hook.

> [We might] as well argue that men cannot be good gynecologists, that only women with children can best understand and administer family law, that only

fat physicians can study obesity, and hungry ones the physiology of starvation as to assert or imply that only people of color or women are uniquely qualified to do justice, wherever relevant, to the place, achievements, and oppressions of minorities and their culture.

Hook's argument, unlike Gertrude Himmelfarb's appeal to "truth, reason, morality, and artistic excellence," is pragmatic: the classics of our culture do have an impact on how we see the world. The greatest works, the works that endure to influence successive generations, are those possessed of the broadest vision—a vision that is progressive if not revolutionary. They challenge our self-image as a society, force us to examine its failings as well as its strengths. And to accomplish this, no minority credentials are required.

What *is* required is a knowledge of the American past. Our

Author Roger Shattuck wants students to learn a core list of books that will inculcate them with America's culture.

schools are now producing a generation that has scarcely heard of the civil rights movement, much less the Civil War, much less the primary documents—the Constitution, the Declaration of Independence, the Bill of Rights—that compose our written heritage. Students are being graduated from our high schools and colleges with no idea who they are or where they're from. In a time when so many of the values that govern our society have eroded, when the channels of transmission—religion, literature, a knowledge of history—no longer function, we're faced with a new phenomenon. The French cultural critic Tzvetan Todorov describes it as "deculturation." We are producing a generation that has no stake in our society; its ways and customs mean nothing to them. And the consequences of this radical alienation are evident in the conditions of near anarchy that prevail in our cities. The fabric of America's social order is wearing thin. Deculturation prefigures disintegration.

What is culture? In a talk given before the American Council of Learned Societies in 1987, Roger Shattuck offered three definitions:

1. Official rituals and ceremonies and celebrations; monuments like the Statue of Liberty; the flag; the national anthem; the pledge of allegiance.

2. A loose, shared store of stories (legendary and historic); folklore (including proverbs); ideas and concepts; historical and presumed facts.

3. A collection of concrete, lasting works (images, buildings, music, writings in poetry and prose) considered significant or revealed or great or beautiful.

Shattuck, author of a study of Proust, a history of Paris literary culture in the 1920s (*The Banquet Years*), and a book about the Wild Boy of Aveyron (*The Forbidden Experiment*), is identified with neither the right nor the left. His mission is to make sure that students learn, that the culture to which he's devoted his life remains intact. The values his definition of culture presupposes—"human continuity, greatness, and recognition of them in masterworks"—are basic to the humanities, key elements of any effort to appreciate a work of art.

They don't answer the objections of New Canonists determined to renovate the curriculum; they simply posit that there *is* a core tradition in the humanities. That core is our cultural legacy. "It is perfectly natural that the tradition one first acquires be that of the country in which one lives," writes Todorov in a recent essay, "How to Fill Those Empty Heads: A Cure for the Humanities Crisis"—"perfectly natural, therefore, that Americans should master the American tradition."

This is E. D. Hirsch's point. What should Americans know? Their own heritage. Why? Because the culture in which they live reflects that heritage. "To teach the ways of one's own community has always been and still remains the essence of the education of our children, who enter neither a narrow tribal culture nor a transcendent world culture but a national literate culture." In support of this contention, Hirsch quotes from the preface to a series of schoolbooks popular at the turn of the century, *Everyday Classics*:

> In an age when the need of socializing and unifying our people is keenly felt, the value of a common stock of knowledge, a common set of ideals, is obvious. A people is best unified by being taught in childhood the best things in its intellectual and moral heritage. Our own heritage is, like our ancestry, composite. Hebrew, Greek, Roman, English, French, and Teutonic elements are blended in our cultural past. . . . An introduction to the best of this is one of our ways of making good citizens.

Why do we study English and American literature? Not to prove the superiority of English culture, or to impose upon minorities a literature that's alien to their experience. We study it, Hirsch explains, "for purely functional reasons," because our literature is the medium through which our language—the essence of our culture—is transmitted and preserved. And to be schooled in that culture, to know one's way around it, is to define our collective identity—as Hirsch puts it, "to decide what 'American' means on the other side of the hyphen in Italo-American or Asian-American."

This is no easy matter. One of the main weaknesses of the American federation of states is that it's such an amalgam of diverse interests and identities. The rhetoric of our primary documents affirms a vision of America to which most of us assent; but they were framed by a dissenting elite for a nation that consisted of a few thousand souls. How are we to address the vastly different constituency that has emerged since the white, male Founding Fathers sat down with their quill pens to compose their manifestos? A lot of troubling developments have interfered with their original vision, notably the absorption of a populace more various and—in the case of blacks and Hispanics—more resistant to assimilation than they could ever have imagined. How should we teach American history and literature? Maybe we should let our students learn these subjects the way earlier generations did—aspiring to become a part of the America they read about. They can decide for themselves where they stand.

Arthur Schlesinger Jr.: "Solid learning must begin with our own origins and tradition."

In his essay "The Opening of the American Mind," Arthur Schlesinger Jr. made a persuasive case for this solution. "For better or for worse," he wrote, "we inherit an American experience, as America inherits a Western experience; and solid learning must begin with our own origins and tradition." We can be critical of that experience. We can fault our society for its racism, its imperialism, its neglect of the soul; we can reject the "cultural relativism" that insists all societies are equal. But whatever one makes of them, the values embodied in the works we teach and in our common rituals are the only ones we have. "History has given them to us," Schlesinger concludes. "They are anchored in our national experience, in our great national documents, in our national heroes, in our folkways, tradition, standards. They work for us; and, for that reason, we live and die by them."

If your work week doesn't end on Friday, Federal Express offers Saturday delivery of your important packages in the U.S.

WE ARE WHAT WE READ

"No one believes in greatness," said Walter Jackson Bate one afternoon when we were talking in his office at Harvard. "That's gone."

I gazed around the professor's comfortable room on the second floor of Warren House. The musty, worn volumes on their varnished shelves exuded an air of vanished civility. I was less than 20 years out of college; it was premature for me to cluck about the crisis in our universities like some patrician, crusty grad, class of '26, in the letters column of the college alumni magazine. But it was hard not to sympathize with Bate's elegiac note. Something had ended. There was no going back.

Was it my own undergraduate days I was nostalgic for, or had the world really changed? A few weeks later, browsing among my books, I stumbled upon this passage in an essay, "Our Age Among the Ages," by John Crowe Ransom:

> Now, I am in the education business, and I can report my observations on that. It is as if a sudden invasion of barbarians had overrun the educational institution. . . . We should not fear them; they are not foreigners, nor our enemies. But in the last resort education is a democratic process, in which the courses are subject to the election of the applicants, and a course even when it has been elected can never rise above the intellectual passion of its pupils, or their comparative indifference. So, with the new generation of students, Milton declines

Harvard professor of English Walter Jackson Bate: "No one believes in greatness. That's gone."

in the curriculum; even Shakespeare has lost heavily; Homer and Virgil are practically gone. The literary interest of the students today is 90 percent in the literature of their own age; more often than not it is found in books which do not find entry into the curriculum, and are beneath the standard which your humble servants, the teachers of literature, are trying to maintain. Chaucer and Spenser and Milton, with their respective contemporaries, will have their existence henceforth in the library, and of course in the love and intimate acquaintance of a certain academic community, and there they will stay except for possible periods when there is a revival of the literature of our own antiquity. Our literary culture for a long time is going to exist in a sprawling fashion, with minority pockets of old-style culture, and some sort of majority culture of a new and indeterminate style. It is a free society, and I should expect that the rights of minorities will be as secure as the rights of individuals.

That was written in 1958.

Once in a while, browsing through the current Harvard catalog as I pursue my curricular research, I come across a course description that stirs me: "The English Bible," for instance, "an introduction to the Hebrew Bible and New Testament with special attention to narrative modes, figures of the human and divine, ethical problems, and sacred mysteries." Or: "The Nineteenth-Century English Novel," billed as "readings in several of the century's major novelists, including Austen, Scott, the Brontës, Dickens, Thackeray, Eliot, Hardy." Even these apparently straightforward offerings haven't escaped a brush with the *Zeitgeist*. The novels aren't simply to be read; they're to be read with an "emphasis on the generic, historical, ideological, and theoretical implications of the texts." Still, books are books. (Or should I say, texts are texts.) Just reading over the authors' names is enough to awaken powerful memories.

It was in a state of intense anticipation that I made my way through this very same catalog each year when it came in the mail toward the end of the summer, a few weeks before the beginning of the fall semester. Then, as now, the catalog was as thick as a 19th-century novel, and crammed with exotic offerings in Sanskrit, Serbo-Croatian, Medieval Greek. How to choose? It was the offerings in English and American literature that compelled my attention. The Reformation, Cromwell, English political philosophy—reading Trevelyan's *History of England* in the cavernous main reading room of Widener Library late at night, the radiators hissing and clanking, the air stale with cigarette smoke (it really *was* a long time ago), I was mesmerized by the power of ideas.

What was this power? How to describe it? Surely I had only the feeblest grasp of the ideas themselves. What did Locke actually mean by natural rights? What was Hobbes's notion of the state? What I remember best is the books themselves, the physical objects, austere pocket-sized volumes in navy blue— *The Communist Manifesto, On Liberty, Areopagitica*—that I still have on my shelves. It was the sheer sensation of learning that excited me, of beginning to master chronology. The blur of names and dates that I found so daunting in September would become, by winter reading period, a coherent narrative. There was *Beowulf, Sir Gawain and the Green Knight,* Chaucer, Spenser, the Elizabethan poets and playwrights, the 17th-century metaphysicals, the neoclassical poets, the Romantics, the Victorians, the Georgians, and finally, the modern poets—the poets I'd read in high school: Eliot and Yeats and Auden. A vivid if disorderly procession that stretched over a thousand years, from England's origins to the present. The moment in which I lived.

How much do I retain now of what I read? Not a great deal. I have faint memories of Emerson's essays, a few lines of Whitman—"I am the man, I suffered, I was there"—a dim awareness of the plot of *Billy Budd* (the sailor hangs). Most of it has vanished. What actually happens in *The Scarlet Letter*? Who was the Faerie Queene?

Nor do I often go back to these books. Sometimes, though, as I hurry past the shelves where they sit in alphabetized rows—the volumes of Virginia Woolf's *Diary*, the Faber editions of T. S. Eliot's prose, the Macmillan edition of Yeats—I find myself thinking back to those winter nights in Widener when I read for no worldly purpose, no hope of gain. When the world expected nothing of me, and my whole purpose in life was to work my way through *The Norton Anthology of English Literature*. At midnight, when the library closed, I would walk out into Harvard Yard, down the icy marble steps, inhaling the crisp New England air, hauling my books in their olive-green canvas book bag back to my dorm, ready to spend the next three hours boning up on the Enclosure Act.

The chronologies, footnotes, and appendixes—all this apparatus of learning—gave scholarly weight to the books I read. They imposed a gloss of erudition. But I always read for the story. What happened next? Racing through Trevelyan's monumental *History of England*, I was enthralled by his dramatic evocation of long ago, "the era of Celt, Saxon, and Dane." This was no dry treatise. A master of English prose, Trevelyan conjured up England from its earliest beginnings, a primitive, ancient world of "giant figures," "warriors at strife," the air reverberant with "the cry of seamen beaching their ships." I've forgotten what domesday was, and whether Henry II came before Richard I. What I remember was realizing how old our civilization is, what a miracle that so much of its history is still intact.

What was that line of Eliot's? *"History is now and England."* But it was also America—America before my time. I read *The Education of Henry Adams*, the three-volume autobiography of Henry James, Malcolm Cowley's *Exile's Return*, the journalism of Edmund Wilson. They weren't the kind of books that made for an education in English literature; they weren't classics. But they gave me a sense of the author's life; they told a story that taught by example. What did they teach? In the largest sense, I suppose, that "the very condition of being human," in Roger Shattuck's words, "is not given but learned." We are what we read. And what better way to establish who we are than to read about others like ourselves—not in the particulars of class or ethnic identity, but in the recognition that we share with them a common heritage?

One of the most striking features of the reading lists I've

come across in various essays and memoirs by American writers is how eclectic they are. There's always been a core of sorts. "When I was an undergraduate in Chicago, we were told not to bother with humanist scholars but to study the Great Books themselves," Saul Bellow recalls. "Bright under-graduates from the slums, the suburbs, or the sticks agreed that the *Phaedrus* or *Hamlet* was exactly what they should be reading." But it was a core expanded by personal predilec-tions, not by politics. Richard Rodriguez, the son of Mexican immigrants, grew up speaking Spanish; the product of a "socially disadvantaged" milieu, he worked his way through Stanford and Columbia and ended up a well-known writer. His memoir, *Hunger of Memory*, is a minor classic, one of the only books I know that describes the American education of a third-world immigrant. What did Rodriguez read as a boy just beginning to grapple with English? Hawthorne's *The Scarlet Letter*, Kipling, *The Babe Ruth Story*, *Moby Dick*, *Gone With the Wind*, *The Good Earth*, and "the entire first volume of the *Encyclopedia Britannica*—A through ANSTEY." What mattered wasn't what one read; it was that one read at all.

Apart from a few hard-liners, no one's demanding that schools institute a uniform curriculum. Whatever conservatives may think, the basic syl-labus can be altered and still survive. "The canon is neither immutable nor totally malleable," insists Tzvetan Todorov. Courses in contemporary literature are nothing new. As long ago as the late 19th century, when William Lyon Phelps, a professor of English at Yale, proposed a course on modern novels, the chairman of the department encouraged him, saying "there was no reason why the literature of 1895 could not be made as suitable a subject for college study as the literature of 1295." And opening up the canon *does* have certain advantages: It teaches us to recognize the existence of cultures other than our own, to endow them with validity. In the end, it makes us tolerant. "To 'decenter' our viewpoint, to break free from egocentric and ethnocentric illusions, we must learn to become detached from ourselves, to see ourselves from the outside," maintains Todorov. "There is only one way to achieve this: by confronting our norms with those of other people, by discovering that they, too, are legitimate."

To hope for a consensus on the curriculum is futile; diversity is the essence of a democratic society. But diversity has its limits. "Even a randomly picked group of intelligent and educated people will agree on a handful of books that everyone should read at some point, in some form," Shattuck asserts. What books? I have neither the authority nor the credentials to put forward a curriculum, but it wouldn't be hard to come up with a provisional list: the standard works by Aristotle and Plato, St. Augustine, Machiavelli, Montaigne, Rousseau, Shakespeare, Milton, Dante; the English political philosophers who inspired those documents that make up the written heritage of our own government; selections from the literature of one European language, read in that language; the King James Bible; and a sample of American literature—as it was before the revisionists arrived on the scene. The Library of America, a series of volumes devoted to reprinting the classics of American literature, has become one of the most significant publishing events of our time. It runs to some 52 volumes so far, in handsome editions unburdened by scholarly apparatus, from the works of Abraham Lincoln to Harriet Beecher Stowe, Ralph Waldo Emerson to Eugene O'Neill, Willa Cather to Henry James. Plans are now afoot to reprint paperback editions of this series: why not adopt them in our schools?

Think of the books we read in high school (my informal poll has turned up a virtually uniform list): *J. B.*, a play by Archibald MacLeish; F. Scott Fitzgerald's *The Great Gatsby*; James Joyce's *Dubliners*; George Eliot's *Silas Marner*; John Steinbeck's *Of Mice and Men*; *Hamlet*; Hemingway's *The Old Man and the Sea*. What do these books have in common? Why are they assigned by high school teachers year after year? They're easy to read, for one thing; they're written with a simplicity and economy that makes them (or made them) readily comprehensible to the average 16-year-old; they're pitched at the right level. But what else? They're stories with what used to be called universal themes; they espouse certain values: perseverance, the consequences of self-betrayal, and responsibility for one's acts. More important, they seem familiar. MacLeish's play is loosely based on the Book of Job; *Hamlet* is perhaps Shakespeare's most accessible play, the great speeches so often quoted they've become part of our everyday language; Hemingway is a showcase of the American vernacular; *Dubliners* has the classic simplicity of a hymn. Is it any wonder that students identify with these books? They're the lore of our culture. This isn't to say we should ignore minority literature, third-world literature, the literature of peoples around the globe. But without a common culture, a culture that possesses certain shared assumptions, there will soon be no America to imagine, no common myth around which to organize our aspirations. The study of American literature invests us in our own society by enabling us to recognize ourselves in it—to find there a general representation of our experience.

What does one learn from these works? That English literature is the primary source of the language that we speak, a living organism, evolved through centuries of use, and thus a repository of our culture's most enduring traditions, the written record of its past. In a practical sense, one also learns the kind of elemental mastery that used to be taken for granted—how to read and write one's own language. (It's not surprising that corporations have begun to recruit humanities majors: they're the only ones who are still literate.)

Sidney Hook, summing up his position on the curricular debate in a 1989 article in *The American Scholar*, listed six things that students "need to know, whether they know it or not." Every student needs to learn how to communicate clearly and effectively, to express himself in a literate way; to have a rudimentary grasp of the natural world, of evolution and genetics; to comprehend the historical, economic, and social forces that have shaped our collective destiny; to know something about religion and morality; to acquire the capacity to reason; and to be "inducted into the cultural legacies of his civilization, its art, literature, and music."

Utopian proposals, perhaps, inspired by a time when Hook

was training the best immigrant minds of his generation at New York University; a time before urban high schools were overwhelmed by crime and drugs; before a population arose that was excluded from any hope of a better life. In a way it seems futile to discuss the curriculum, to debate which books students ought to read, when in most inner-city schools few of them can read at all. But even at the university level, few believe any longer in Hook's basic propositions. Harvard's core curriculum is a case in point. Adopted after much debate, it concedes—I quote from the 1989 catalog—that its charges should be "broadly educated," then goes on to stipulate that "it does not define intellectual breadth as the mastery of a set of Great Books, or the digestion of a specific quantum of information, or the surveying of current knowledge in certain fields. Rather, the Core seeks to introduce students to the major approaches to knowledge in areas that the faculty considers indispensable to undergraduate education."

The virtue of this approach is that it enables students to acquire what Hook calls "methodological sophistication." But it seems an odd way to go about things now. Our culture is beset by an epidemic of collective amnesia. I know less than the generation of college students before me did, and the generation after me knows even less. We've suffered what novelist Cynthia Ozick, lamenting the decline of T. S. Eliot's reputation, describes as a "cultural autolobotomy." Not only is the literary tradition Eliot represented gone from the scene, but the very idea of tradition has become obsolete. Who cares about "approaches to knowledge" in such a crisis situation? If we as a society can't agree that there is a body of knowledge to be mastered, much less what that body is, our very continuance as a literate culture will be in doubt. "If we do not provide adequate knowledge to fill those hungry minds and empty schoolroom hours, something else will," warns Shattuck. "That something else may well be deadening and corrupting—estrangement, anomie, idle vandalism, drugs, crime, suicide. These things cannot be said too often."

Saving our schools isn't just a matter of improving test scores or teaching children to read. There has to be a vision of what it is we wish them to know. Yale's black-studies pro-

In the early '70s, Federal Express pioneered overnight
air express in the U.S. Today, Federal Express offers reliable document,
package and freight delivery worldwide.

gram is in disarray: several members of the department have defected, and those who remain lack a sense of purpose or direction. Why is this? In part because they can't agree on what to study. There are courses of instruction in the Hausa, Yoruba, and Zulu languages; Swahili literature; and "Psychological Perspectives on African-American Experiences in the United States." The field is wide—inchoate, the faculty complains. Furthermore, it tends to attract minority students, fostering a kind of unintentional segregation. Only now, some 20 years after the founding of Afro-American studies, are the consequences of this policy becoming clear. In jettisoning the idea of a canon of Great Books, we've undermined what used to be our primary educational goal: the transmisson of a body of works arrived at through decades, even centuries of debate. "We're still at the point of resurrecting texts," says Henry Louis Gates, who is busy establishing a canon of his own with *The Norton Anthology of Afro-American Literature*. "We have to produce the tradition, *then* we have to analyze it." That's all well and good; but why not read the tradition that's there?

It's pointless to sit around wishing that everyone would just get down to work and read the classics. Things have gone too far. The curricular revolution is entrenched; the students are militant; the class of educated citizens that once prided itself on a knowledge of European culture has dwindled to nothing. No one has described the situation with more elegiac fervor than Cynthia Ozick: "High art is dead. The passion for inheritance is dead. Tradition is equated with obscurantism. The wall that divided serious high culture from the popular arts is breached; anything can count as 'text.'"

In the generation to come, there won't even be an audience for this art. The "Anglo-Saxon cultural values" decried in the Sobol report no longer exist. The bow-tied English professors who promoted them have all gone into the dark. As the critic David Rieff, a clear-eyed radical, says with some acerbity, "Whatever the future is, it isn't white."

How to educate this new generation will be a matter of debate. What's essential is to preserve and affirm the idea of basic literacy, of learning grounded in a core of knowledge.

Bloom derides Mortimer Adler, founder of the Great Books idea at the University of Chicago, as an equal-opportunity intellectual, but when Adler shows up at Goldblatt Elementary School on the city's destitute West Side to conduct a seminar on *Hamlet* with children from the housing projects, he's working on behalf of what has always been a crucial element in the American dream: culture as a path to self-improvement. My grandmother had on the shelf in her television room Pelican paperbacks of Kant and Kierkegaard. I have no idea what she made of them, but I'm sure something got through, even if it was only the idea that there were ideas. To be thoroughly modern, to be an American, was to know about these books—to be educated. The mere possession of them was a sign that she'd arrived.

Why did Allan Bloom and E. D. Hirsch become the intellectual superstars of the late 1980s? The tremendous commercial success of their books reflected this hunger to learn. But they also had a message. They had discovered a potential threat to our society and gave warning. America is foundering because Americans no longer get a proper education. In their attempts to redress injustice, the radicals of the 1960s unwittingly helped to perpetuate it; the assault on the curriculum has undermined the foundation of learning on which our society rests. The problem could be simply put: What we don't know will hurt us. And it has.

In style, these two prophets of cultural doom could hardly be more unalike. Hirsch is the practical one: his book is a primer on how to make our educational system work. Hirsch's Cultural Literacy Foundation, his textbook series, and his newly published *Dictionary of Cultural Literacy* are designed to get results. Bloom is more theoretical: his book appeals to the perennial student in us—that yearning, after years out in the busy world, to restore for a brief moment the innocence of our undergraduate days, the long nights in the library spent struggling through *The Social Contract*. In the end, *The Closing of the American Mind* is about the joys of education: how to live in the world without losing one's soul.

Hirsch is a booster. He wants America to be great again, and to assert its greatness as a culture. Bloom likes the political opportunities America affords and holds its culture in contempt. But their basic message is the same. "Just as in politics the responsibility for the fate of freedom in the world has devolved upon our regime, so the fate of philosophy in the world has devolved upon our universities, and the two are related as they have never been before," writes Bloom on the last page of his book. "The gravity of our given task is great, and it is very much in doubt how the future will judge our stewardship." By "philosophy," I take it, Bloom means the humanities. What we read, he's saying—*if* we read—will determine America's fate.

This can all seem very abstract, despite the urgency with which our two prophets deliver the bad news. What do the Great Books have to do with the fragile edifice of culture? Doesn't it always need shoring up against the forces of barbarism? To my mind, the connection isn't fanciful. The new curriculum is an effort to validate the claims of the individual. But what about the claims of society? Who will argue on its behalf? Only a nation schooled in basic values—and we're no longer a nation schooled in anything at all—will grasp the negotiation between personal freedom and collective self-interest that is the essence of our American democracy. Those ideas are learned in books. The Great Books. The best that has been thought and said. The canon.

Until a few years ago, this was our educational mandate. If it goes, a tradition that we cherished will go with it.

In the air or on the ground, Federal Express is working to meet the needs of business throughout the world.

Additional Copies

To order additional copies of *The Book Wars*
for friends or colleagues, please write to
The Larger Agenda Series, Whittle Direct Books,
505 Market St., Knoxville, Tenn. 37902.

For a single copy, please enclose a check for $11.95
payable to The Larger Agenda Series. When
ordering 10 or more books, enclose $9.95 for
each; for orders of 50 or more books, enclose
$7.95 for each. If you wish to place an order by
phone, call 800-284-1956.

Also available, at the same prices, are copies
of the previous books in The Larger Agenda Series:
The Trouble With Money by William Greider,
Adhocracy: The Power to Change
by Robert H. Waterman Jr., and
Life After Television by George Gilder.

Please allow two weeks for delivery.
Tennessee residents must add 7¾ percent sales tax.